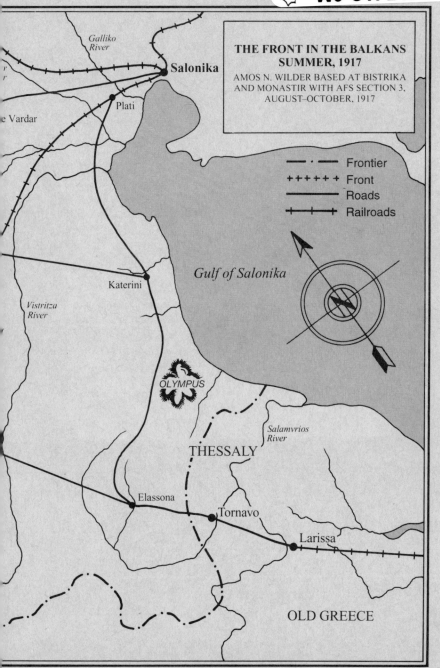

**THE FRONT IN THE BALKANS
SUMMER, 1917**

AMOS N. WILDER BASED AT BISTRIKA
AND MONASTIR WITH AFS SECTION 3,
AUGUST–OCTOBER, 1917

— · — · — Frontier
+ + + + + + Front
————— Roads
+—+—+—+ Railroads

*Galliko
River*

Salonika

Plati

e Vardar

Katerini

Gulf of Salonika

*Vistritza
River*

OLYMPUS

*Salamvrios
River*

THESSALY

Elassona

Tornavo

Larissa

OLD GREECE

SINCE
1854

MECHANICS' INSTITUTE

LIBRARY & CHESS ROOM

57 Post Street, San Francisco, CA 94104
(415) 393-0101

* * *

Armageddon Revisited

* * *

Armageddon Revisited

A World War I Journal

Amos N. Wilder

Yale University Press

New Haven and London

Designed by Nancy Ovedovitz and set in Bodoni type by Tseng Information Systems, Durham, North Carolina. Printed in the United States of America by Book Crafters, Inc., Chelsea, Michigan

Library of Congress Cataloging-in-Publication Data
Wilder, Amos Niven, 1895–1993
    Armageddon revisited : a World War I journal / Amos N. Wilder.
    p.   cm.
    Includes bibliographical references and index.
    ISBN 0-300-05560-9 (alk. paper)
    1. Wilder, Amos Niven, 1895–1993.   2. World War, 1914–1918—Personal narratives, American.   3. Soldiers—United States—Biography.
4. United States.   Army—Biography.   I. Title.
D640.W578   1994
940.4'8173—dc20   93-33296
                      CIP

A catalogue record for this book is available from the British Library.

The paper in this book meets the guidelines for permanence and durability of the Committee on Production Guidelines for Book Longevity of the Council on Library Resources.

10   9   8   7   6   5   4   3   2   1

This book is dedicated in homage to David Jones, unrivaled poet and mythographer of the Great War. In his *In Parenthesis* he was able to read our ordeals in the light of ancient prototypes, prodigies, and vindications and thus to reveal the deeper meaning of our experience as it was overruled for higher ends.

I also dedicate this book to A. T. W. and J. G. W., my grandchildren, with the thought that the past has its afterlife in the hearts of succeeding generations, and we retrieve what we can of its overt happening and thus orient ourselves to its deeper intentions.

✳ ✳ ✳

Contents

* * *

Acknowledgments

I am especially indebted to Missy Daniel of Boston for her interest in this book.

I also wish to thank William R. Crout for his extensive transcription of my texts and knowledgeable help and his never-failing personal kindnesses.

Special thanks are also due to Pamela Jaques for her skillful deciphering of some of my now ancient jottings and her use of the computer to move these texts one further step to contemporary availability.

I must also thank my wife, Catharine, whose strategies as homemaker have been called upon in addition to those as intermediary and communicator.

I wish to acknowledge with thanks the editor and publisher of George Panichas (ed.), *Promise of Greatness: The War of 1914–1918* (New York: John Day, 1968), a symposium which included my contribution, "At the Nethermost Piers of History: World War I, A View from the Ranks," which I have cited in this book.

My thanks also go to my son Tappan for his inestimable services.

* * *

Chronology of Amos N. Wilder's

World War I Service

1916

26 September	Enlists in New York as volunteer ambulance driver
21 October	Sails for France
6 November	Begins three-month assignment, American Ambulance Hospital in Paris ("the Paris Service")

1917

31 January	Transfers to American Field Service (AFS)
7 February	Begins three-month assignment, AFS Section 2, at the front in the Argonne, west of Verdun
6 April	United States enters war against Germany
16 May	Begins seven-day leave in London and the Lake District
7 July	Following reenlistment in AFS, departs Paris for Macedonia and service with the Army of the Orient
3 August	Begins assignment with AFS Section 3, attached to Second Serbian Division, encamped at Bistrika, Serbian Front

19 October	Departs Salonika for Paris
15 November	Released from AFS in Paris
26 November	Enlists in Paris as private in U.S. Army, assigned to Field Artillery Training School, Valdahon

1918

2 January	Reassigned at Valdahon to A Battery, Seventeenth Field Artillery, Second Division; promoted to corporal
8 March	Departs Valdahon for the front, Rupt Sector, southeast of Verdun
1 June	Division rushed to Château-Thierry/Belleau Wood defense to repel massive German thrust toward the Marne and Paris
7–8 July	Regiment placed in reserve during Second Battle of the Marne
15 July	Begins forced march for Soissons/Viller-Cotterets mobilization and decisive attack of 18 July
29 July	Division rusticated near Nancy
Sept.–October	Hospitalization, convalescent camps, influenza quarantine in southwest France
12–13 Sept	American-led victory at St.-Mihiel
20 October	Returns to A Battery behind the front at Blanc Mont Ridge
31 October	Moves to the front in Argonne Forest for attack of 1–2 November
8 November	Foch gives terms with 72-hour armistice for German answer
11 November	Armistice officially declared

1919

28 June	Discharged from the U.S. Army at Gievres Discharge Depot after duties at Bendorf and Coblenz with the Army of Occupation and release for studies at University of Toulouse
September	Begins senior year at Yale

✳ ✳ ✳

Biographical and
Editorial Note

Amos N. Wilder was born on September 18, 1895 in Madison, Wisconsin. In 1916 his family had recently moved to New Haven following his father's postings as American consul general in Hong Kong and Shanghai from 1906 to 1915.

The author with his brother and three sisters constituted a family of writers: Thornton (playwright and novelist), Charlotte (winner of the Shelley Memorial Award for Poetry), Isabel (graduate of the Yale School of Drama and novelist), and Janet Dakin (scientist who wrote on conservation and equestrian topics).

After attending public schools in Madison and Berkeley, California (with brief schooling in China), Amos Wilder prepared for college at the Thacher school in Ojai, California. After two years at Oberlin he transferred to Yale in the fall of 1915. Following the war he received his B.A., B.D., and Ph.D. from Yale. He was ordained in 1926 and for several years served as minister of the First Congregational Church in North Conway, New Hampshire.

In 1930, Amos Wilder began his teaching and scholarly career at

Hamilton College. He subsequently taught at Andover Newton Theological School, Chicago Theological Seminary and Federated Theological Faculty, University of Frankfort, and Harvard Divinity School, where he retired as Hollis Professor of Divinity Emeritus in 1963.

Despite poor health in his later years Amos Wilder retained to his death a zest for the several elements that comprised his professional career and related interests—New Testament studies, the relation between religion and the arts, literary criticism, and the practice of poetry. The summer before he died he was still able to spend part of many days in his "summer workshop," a rudimentary cabin in the woods in Blue Hill Falls, Maine. It was here that much of the work was done on the great project of his last years, the writing of this book, which he completed in April 1992. He used a typewriter ardently in the manner taught by his journalist father as well as by this time a reading machine that allowed him to read despite near total blindness.

Amos Wilder died on May 1, 1993. Anticipating the end, he asked me to serve as his surrogate in dealing with the inevitable queries in the final editing, adding with characteristic modesty that he hoped that it would not be a burden. It has not been a burden; rather, it has been a delight and a privilege.

Changes made to the text since the author's death include the deletion of a few repetitions and a slight reorganization of parts of the text in order to maintain the continuity of the narrative. Robin Gibbs Wilder and William R. Crout have been helpful in making judgments about these changes.

Extreme care has been given to preserve the integrity of the extracts taken from Amos Wilder's journal. Sometimes writing under extraordinary constraints—in his dugout during bombardments, for example—he often compressed language to save both paper and time. Only changes necessary for clarity, such as spelling out certain abbreviations, have been made. In some cases the author himself added words of explanation in brackets. In the final editing a few additional lines from the journal have been added to several entries as well as footnotes containing information that may be helpful to the reader. All names, places, dates, and citations have been checked for accuracy to the extent possible, and the few errors or imprecisions have been corrected.

I extend special thanks to Patricia Barry for helping me with a line-by-line review of the extracts against the original sources and to William L. Foley for responding graciously to queries about the American Field Service experience in World War I. It has also been a great pleasure to work with Harriett Blood on the maps, which are based on Field Service maps published in 1920. The Western front map was modified to reflect the author's experience in the U.S. Army. All the pictures reproduced in this book were taken by the author or through the lens of his Brownie camera. (A stylus feature, which permitted the photographer to write on each negative, has allowed most pictures to be identified quite precisely.)

I deeply regret that my father did not have the opportunity to meet and work with Jonathan Brent, the acquisitions editor at Yale University Press, and Noreen O'Connor-Abel, the book's thoughtful and skillful manuscript editor. Had he done so their names would hold a prominent place in his acknowledgments—where they rightly deserve to be.

A. Tappan Wilder

＊ ＊ ＊

Prologue

The American Field Service had its genesis in 1914 in the activities
of the civilian American Hospital in Paris. In response to the emergency created by the first Battle of the Marne in 1914–1915, initiatives
were taken to assist the French in caring for the casualties that crowded
the available hospitals. In this period the hospital's medical and ambulance services also became associated with convalescent centers near
Paris organized by American friends like the Whitneys, Vanderbilts,
and Nortons. These efforts were deeply informed by a significant out-
burst of Francophile sentiment in the American colony in Paris.

In 1915, the still uncompleted Lycée Pasteur in Neuilly was taken over
by the American Hospital, multiplying many times the available accommodations and becoming the headquarters of what was known as the
"Paris Service," an ambulance corps manned largely by young American volunteers driving Buicks. This service became so experienced and
trusted that the French authorities assigned to it the tasks of meeting the
hospital trains arriving from the front at the Gare de la Chapelle and dis-
tributing the casualties to some 400 hospital sites throughout the city.

In conjunction with the Paris Service, the American Field Service (AFS) emerged in the winter of 1914–1915. By April 1915 three fully organized sections were attached to French divisions, one near Dunkirk, one in the Lorraine, and one in the Vosges. During the summer of 1916 a headquarters for this development was established in Passy at 21 rue Raynouard. Loaned for the duration, this handsome property with its chateau, offices, accommodations, parking lot, and infirmary became the quasi-legendary home of the AFS for hundreds of volunteers, going and coming. Appeals for drivers and for cars—the Model-T Ford had now become the vehicle of choice—were widely publicized in America, especially in our colleges and universities.

By the late summer of 1917 the AFS had thirty-four ambulance sections, each with twenty cars, serving with as many French divisions, including fourteen transport sections of camions delivering munitions and supplies to the front. When the American army took over the entire operation in October 1917, some 2,500 young men, largely college students, were serving or had served as drivers.[1]

By November 1916 when I reached Paris there were, therefore, already hundreds of American students who had similarly volunteered to serve in the American Field Service as ambulance drivers with the French, well before the American declaration of war. Instead of returning to Yale for my senior year I had signed on at the New York office of the Service for a six-month engagement. Our campuses had been hearing about this opportunity for some time, and many schools and communities had contributed cars and raised funds for the program.

I recorded details of my enlistment in the Ambulance Service in what I then called my War Diary. Its first entry is dated "New Haven, Oct. 6th, 1916." These entries also cover my journey through England to France and, finally, to Paris.

On my twenty-first birthday Papa threw out another hint concerning the American Ambulance. I said nothing about it until the next day, though I thought much. I then took him up on it and said I wanted to go. The best thing in these dilemmas is to do the extraordinary thing. Father's application to the New York office and Dean [Frederick Sheetz] Jones' note drew an invitation to call. We called

Tuesday, Sept. 26, and Mr. Hereford accepted me. We chose the Paris Service for a starter. After looking over the Y.M.C.A. auto school in N.Y., I decided to take Tom O'Connor's course at the Depot Garage in New Haven.

N. Y. Fri. Oct. 20

Left the house at seven this morning. Father and I visited the Ambulance office and the English and French consuls. We had a last dinner at a garden restaurant on 49th St and I saw "Hush" played at the "Little Theatre."

London, Nov. 2

Sailed from N. Y. on the St. Paul, Oct. 21 and reached Liverpool Sunday Oct. 29. . . . The first thing I did in London was to go to Westminster Abbey, where I was just in time for the 10 A.M. service. It was the regular morning prayers from the prayer book. But in Westminster Abbey. And with all the men in the choir gone and only the boys left. And with soldiers in uniform from over the seas—Canadians, Australians, and wounded English soldiers, listening, shy in the background. . . . Needless to say, the solemnity that the ever-imminent war cast over the service could not but deepen the experience. . . .

I visited the sacred "Centre Court" at the tennis grounds at Wimbledon and talked with the care-taker about the sensation that Maurice McLoughlin made when he played there. The place was deserted and the notices of the Davis Cup matches of Aug. 1914 still fading away on the walls.

At this time I would have been very much surprised if I had been told that I would play on this same court in 1922 with my Oxford partner, Charles Kingsley.*

---

*Amos Wilder was a rising tennis player in 1916. Thus his interest in seeing Wimbledon stadium—where matches had been suspended for the duration. In 1920, Wilder won the intercollegiate doubles title with his Yale partner, Lee Wiley. Wilder and Kingsley lost a Centre Court match in 1922 against the eventual winners of the title, Australians Randolph Lysett and J. O. Anderson. A survey of his tennis career, including observations about the influence of World

London, Nov. 4 '16

Today I received my credentials for passing across the channel
and to Paris via Southampton, Le Havre.

Paris, Thur. Nov. 9

After a brief delay caused by the military authorities and cus-
toms, we got aboard the Vera at Southampton about 10:30 P.M.
Sun. the 5th. We were in Le Havre before dawn. At the dock there
were small craft about us. One of them had been mismanaged, col-
lided forcibly with us, and then drifted into other difficulties. The
Frenchmen on board jabbered and gesticulated without seeming
to get anywhere. An hour later, the last we saw of them, they were
afoul of an anchor-chain and they may be running to and fro on her
still. My first view of French efficiency. . . . I got into Paris Monday
night, Nov. 6th.

Because of my diffidence as regards derring-do and my inexperience
with driving, it was agreed that my initial three months should be spent
with what was called the Paris Service in Neuilly—before going to the
front. Indeed, I was as unfamiliar with first aid to motor cars as to casualties at an advanced dressing station.

Paris, like all foreign capitals, had long had its American colony.
These Francophiles had not been slow in 1914 in offering their aid to the
beleaguered capital, and not least prompt were the patrons and staff of
the American Hospital and their medical and ambulance services associated with convalescent centers near Paris.

Although the ambulance service was not formally a belligerent corps
—our cars had Red Cross identifications—the drivers were linked with
both the French automotive and medical corps and received the rations
and daily five-cents pay (commonly waived) of French privates. Our volunteer status was distinguished by our officer-like uniforms with khaki
tunics, Sam Brown belts, and whipcord breeches.

In crossing the sea for this kind of exposed activity we had a sense of
high adventure, with many analogies to a pioneering, crusading spirit,

War I on it, is found in Amos N. Wilder, "A Game to Remember: Recollections
of a Bygone Era," *Racquet* 7, No. 3 (Summer 1988), pp. 62–75.

struggling with Utopian hopes left us by our New World predecessors. As it turned out, our venture led us into many of the dramas of the great conflict, and we in the Field Service also had our perils and casualties.

My three months with the Paris Service in the winter of 1916–1917 gave me a different first experience and memory of Paris than those we today associate with visiting as a tourist or student. This was a city at war. Not long before, the common taxis of the streets had been called on to save the city by rushing troops to the front—at the doors of the city— during the Battle of the Marne. Hostile planes were sometimes overhead. Our cars on one occasion rushed to a conflagration where a Big Bertha had exploded. The casualties of all ranks whom we delivered to the hospitals—sometimes in Versailles, at the Hôtel-Dieu, or right on the Champs Elysées at the Petit Palais—came from every part of France and had been wounded on many fronts.

We drivers of this Paris squad had our meals at the Lycée Pasteur but were housed some blocks away in the high-ceilinged rooms of "the Chateau." This was a formal residence whose ornate iron gates leading to the Bois de Boulogne were always locked.

Until I received my uniform and had passed my driving test I could only assist the other drivers and work on the cars. All those not on scheduled duty were in any case free to move about the city. We were expected, however, to telephone in every hour or so in case a call had come in requiring an entire section of cars to be on hand at the station for the arrival of a trainload of casualties. Since this inquiry had to be made in French to the hospital switchboard ("Est-ce qu'il y a un appel?"), we had quite a lot of difficulty keeping in touch.

On my arrival at the Chateau I found an unoccupied room and emptied out my father's old Gladstone bag in a corner. This capacious and now crushed leather carryall had served him for years in China during his consular duties. After I received my uniform, the bag held my civilian belongings for almost three years while I was soldiering in France, Macedonia, and the Rhineland. As my link with home and peacetime pursuits it was stored first in Neuilly, then in Passy when I was with the Field Service, and finally at the American Express Company when I was with our American forces.

A soldier, like a monk or convict, can have very little baggage or property of his own. His very identity is changed or attenuated when he puts on a uniform. In the army his free will falls under the chain of command. Save for the original act of consent he becomes a statistic, and his identity shrinks to the dog tag or number hung around his neck, all that identifies him among those retrieved after battle.

In the ambulance service we did not leave our civilian life so far behind. In Paris, of course, we had access to bank accounts, shops, and civilian postal service. In the Field Service a camera was allowed. I could always set up a dark room and develop my own film and prints. When I joined the army proper I left my Brownie camera and other valuables in the Gladstone bag as a pledge of my eventual return to peacetime occupations.

No doubt the motives which led so many of us to join the Field Service were varied. The main idea, as with the aviators of the Lafayette Escadrille, was to be where the action was, and with this was mixed the romance of adventure. The urge of the Francophile also played no small part. An early appeal of the Field Service for volunteers began with the words of Joffre: "The United States of America have not forgotten that the first page of the history of their independence was written with a little of the blood of France." There was an increasing sentiment, moreover, that America should be in the war. In the summer of 1916 I had been on the staff at a boys' training camp at Fort Terry on Plum Island off New London, Connecticut, and had heard Theodore Roosevelt fulminate to the ranks of teenagers on the disgrace of our delay.

More significant to me as one concerned with the issues of pacifism and the moral aspects of the war was my experience as a student at Oberlin College in 1914–1915. President Henry Churchill King in his large Sunday class dealt for many months with the origins of the war, an analysis of Prussianism, traditional Christian views of church and state, and historical Christian attitudes to war. The upshot was, in effect, justification of America's participation with the Allies. No doubt King did not know some of the things about the background of the war which were brought out later by historians like Sidney Fay. In any case, the lurid tales of German atrocities were not part of the argument.

King, like myself, was a Congregationalist and with Oberlin as a whole represented the tradition of the abolitionists and of the New England theocrats, according to which the church associates itself with the moral responsibility of the state. The same Calvinist tradition led Woodrow Wilson later to select the term "covenant," which had been used by John Calvin for the ordering of Geneva (not to mention the Scotch and English Covenanters) for the instrument of the League of Nations. In the spring of 1919 when the Army of Occupation in Germany released many of us college men to attend French and British universities, I was in the Army School Detachment at the University of Toulouse. Several of us interested in the Christian ministry were assigned to the nearby old French Huguenot seminary at Montauban. The Dean, Emile Doumergue (kin to Gaston Doumergue, who was later president of France), was the greatest Calvin biographer and scholar of the time. He took immense delight in recognizing the link between the Geneva of John Calvin and the political and international idealism of Wilson, son of a Presbyterian manse.

It is all too easy to oversimplify the motives of the combatants in the Great War, as in any war. This bears on the familiar appeals and inducements associated with "propaganda" and jingoism or shallower versions of patriotism. One should recognize the great differences of maturity, perspective, and commitment of those involved. The anonymous soldiery, moreover, are commonly inarticulate, but their collaboration may often be animated by deeper fealties than those generally invoked. The cause of the preservation of European civilization transcended that of any narrow patriotism. Here also any overly facile appeals to the slogans of the American and French Revolutions could find a sobering corrective. Thus those Americans who volunteered to serve in the American Field Service might have found it difficult to identify their motives just because they were reluctant to reduce them to any kind of calculus. Those kinds of imponderable considerations which operated were not congenial to a litany of familiar appeals.

Nevertheless, there was, as I have said, a great diversity of outlook and witness, as among the combatants generally. One invaluable feature of the Field Service was that its sections were made up of many of the most alert and gifted students of our colleges and this set a standard of noblesse oblige for our national mobilization and its spirit later.

A parallel to this role of an elite youth in the war is found in the writing of the French writer Henry de Montherlant. The first of his books dealing with his war experience is entitled *Le Relève du matin* (literally, The changing of the guard at dawn). Referring to the promptness and final sacrifice of almost all the members of his Catholic preparatory school, his elegy celebrates their total commitment and their faithfulness to the moral and patriotic code of their elite tradition.

Thus when it came to motivation of whatever elements and ranks in the armed forces, one should recognize the leavening influence of those with a more grounded perception of the issues at stake and a more enlightened dedication.

Americans who were in Europe before our declaration of war encountered bitterness over our delay. Passing through London on my way to the Continent in October, 1916, I heard one music-hall comedian observe that George Washington "never let a lie slip through his teeth." "Yes," was the answer, "because like all Americans he spoke through his nose." But the disparagement, at least of American civilians, continued after the war in France, and sometimes for good reasons. In his *Chant funèbre pour les morts de Verdun,* Henry de Montherlant exclaims at the sacrilege of the first American tourists of the Verdun battle fields who carried off skulls in the trunks of their cars. "Peoples without a past need souvenirs. Already Washington used to exhibit piously one of the supposed keys to the Bastille, which actually were fabricated at Paris by the dozen."[2] But the American vanguard in France was honored, often in embarrassing ways. Arriving from the front with soiled uniform and, no doubt, marks of fatigue, I was offered a seat by a Frenchwoman in the crowded métro. The perennial irritations between Americans and the French at the superficial levels of politics and tourism do not touch the deep confraternity in arms of the anonymous combatants in the ranks.

For the purposes of this chronicle I have disinterred from old trunks and cartons the letters I wrote home from France and Serbia, not looked at for many years. Most of them were written on the cheap lined sheets picked up in a village *papetrie.* Correspondence from the Field Service includes the official French postcard designated "Correspondence mili-

taire" and sometimes carries the surcharge "Contrôle postal militaire."
One envelope was stamped RECEIVED WITHOUT CONTENTS, N.Y.P.Q.,
PENN. TERM. STA. After I transferred to the U.S. Army the letterhead of
the YMCA often appears with its red triangle and ON SERVICE WITH THE
AMERICAN EXPEDITIONARY FORCES, or that of the Knights of Columbus
with its emblem and the American flag in color. From this time on each
letter was censored and signed thus: "John Smith, Lt. 17th F.A." The
envelopes carry the seals U.S. ARMY POSTAL SERVICE and A.E.F. PASSED
AS CENSORED, again with the signature, which after all these years reminds me of the names of the several officers of my battery.

Army letters were often written in a dugout at night by the light of
the little lamps which like our briquets the French had taught us to im-
provise. With a small can and kerosene parleyed from a camion driver,
supplemented by a strip of cloth for a wick and a sawed-off cartridge, one
had a flare that would burn for hours. Books could not be sent through
Army mail to the front, but my family tore the covers off them and sent
them rolled up like magazines. My letters carry a running comment on
classics thus available.

The narrative which follows comes from wartime letters as well as the
journal I kept from late 1916 to my discharge in 1919. Jotted down under
pressure of the moment, these entries vary in form from the highly condensed and fragmentary to the expansive. Because I was thinking of my
family at home I tended to write of what would interest them. In fact I find
that the letters I wrote home often echo or amplify my journal of the time.

My father, who had been a journalist in New Haven, arranged to have
extended excerpts from my letters home published in the *New Haven
Journal-Courier* (of which he was later associate editor) and other periodicals. Thus in addition to my journal, which in parts had become very
hard to decipher, I could recur to these many pages of my letters which
my father had mounted for possible future use, having carefully retained
the dates of the letters. These family letters thus had some wider eva-
nescent circulation during the war itself.

In addition to the letters, other memorabilia came to light during the
preparation of this book: a receipt for $25 from a New Haven garage for
a "Course in automobile repair and driving"; a Paris driving license,

dated November 28, 1916 (my driving test was on the Champs Elysées); every kind of identity card, *permis de séjour, ordre de mouvement*—including records of the tour de force of red tape overcome for permission to spend a week's leave in the Lake District, wangled from both civil and military authorities, French and British, as well as the American Embassy in Paris. There is a receipt from "Lloyd & Co., High Class English Tailors," place de la Madeleine, for my ambulance uniform, "tunic, breeches and insignia"; an inventory of equipment received when enlisting in the Field Artillery; a penciled plan of a small French village indicating billeting arrangements for A Battery: officers, men, picket lines, infirmary, pumps for drinking water. A printed set of rules handed to men on leave in Paris included as No. 7: "The Military Police have been ordered to take the names and report all ranks, including Militarized Civilians, who permit themselves to be solicited on the streets."

Even the most trifling of such items gratify by their concreteness. The past seems less vague. So the historian cherishes his papyri fragments, coins, and graffiti. Sometimes such archives have more importance. I found the original of a traced firing mission for batteries of our regiment indicating the successive advances of a creeping barrage, by minutes, in the area of Belleau Wood (duly deposited with the historical section of the 2nd Division).

Various aspects of our experience in the Paris Service further evoke our rapid initiation. The original wounding or maiming or gassing most often took place in some advanced trench or exposed crossroad or staging area. Here the Field Service had its part to play. Brought to his ambulance by stretcher-bearer—and the car might well be waiting at a "dugout" serving as a *poste de secours*—the wounded man would then be driven to a field hospital. Then after further first aid he would be taken, whether as a sitting or stretcher case, to a base hospital, very likely at a railhead. Thus he might eventually be sent on to Paris or Lyons or Tours.

Once at a *poste de secours* in the Argonne we had a shell-shocked *poilu* (colloquial term for French soldier). He was distracted, and we could not very well drive him in the enclosed vehicle with other casualties. It was decided that I should leave my car there at the *poste* and be shut in with the poor fellow for the somewhat extended trip to a railhead hospital (at St. Ménéhould). In the obscurity of the ambulance (with only a small window to look back through) our driver could not really observe our behavior, nor for that matter, my safety! My companion muttered, stared, and jerked, but his first transport from the front was thus successful.

Meeting the hospital trains involved a sequence of dramas. First was our prompt mobilization in the Neuilly hospital court and ·the speedy procession of twenty or more heavy ambulances across Paris from west to east. Our chief rivals in the skills of the road were the Paris taxi drivers, and they were not supposed to cut through our file. If they so presumed they were considered fair game for reprisal. Some of our drivers claimed to have neatly taken off the wheel of such an offender's car.

The second drama was at the Gare de la Chapelle, a large freight station near the Gare du Nord whose floor spaces were adapted as though for hospital wards. The long trains with the wounded in them on superposed stretchers would pull in to the platform, and we Americans (rather than the old French "territorials" or reservists) would move the casualties on their stretchers to the great hall where nurses would busy themselves with their dressings and where food and beverages were distributed. Meanwhile, doctors were classifying the men and assigning them to appropriate hospitals.

This introduced what was for us the third drama. Each driver was given a *fiche* which inventoried his "cases" as *couché* (lying) or *assis* (sitters) and how many; the time; and the hospital to which the men were to be delivered.

After our charges had been led or wheeled away, we drivers then had the pleasure of being served coffee by the French staff who had received us. As on later similar occasions at dressing-stations in dugouts near the front lines, these circumstances would lead to delightful Franco-American interplay and bonhomie.

The hospital trains seemed most often to arrive in Paris at night. We had the impression that this was intentional so that this evidence of the havoc of the war would be to some extent minimized in the city. In any case we often had to find our way in the small hours of the night to the hospital indicated. The French provided *gendarmes* to help us find the way. Our drivers took pride in often dispensing with this aid, once we had come to know the old city and its *banlieue*.

My months in Paris occasioned further instructive involvements. I found an old French teacher who drilled me in the language and made me memorize poems of Victor Hugo and Lamartine to which I still recur on sleepless nights. There was at this time a well-known Abbé Felix Klein, a spiritual director who visited the American Hospital. He introduced me to a young engineer, Alfred Chochod, who was exempt from military service because of his position in a munitions factory in Surveiliers. We exchanged language instruction in frequent conversations, but I most valued this friend as an example of a French Catholic type of discipline and piety. In introducing us the abbé was hesitant lest the worldly American Protestant might corrupt his model charge. He was all the more puzzled, if not reassured, when he found that I had my own Puritan code which included at that time abstinence from wine!

The Paris service assigned four or five of its ambulances regularly for a week or more to duties at Mrs. H. Payne Whitney's hospital in Juilly, thirty or forty miles north of Paris. The property was a picturesque old walled school once attended by Napoleon's brother. All around it were vivid reminders of the Battle of the Marne in 1914, perforated walls for sharpshooters and scattered burial sites with their hasty identifications of the slain, French and German. At this hospital I met a young Belgian lieutenant, Jules Deschamps, who became my friend for life. He was then an X-ray assistant on the staff. He served during most of the war in the Belgian artillery. His home in Tournai, with much of the city and its famous cathedral, had been badly damaged in 1914 when the Germans captured the city. Deschamps later became the leading citizen of Tournai and its presiding judge. He also directed the restoration of countless features of the old city which had at one time been the capital of France.

Here was another kind of Catholic for my education. Once a *libre-penseur*, he was a man whose outlook was saturated with the aesthetic and intellectual culture of the Continent. From our first meeting he guided me in my reading of French letters. He also introduced me, in the area of social services, to the merciful institution of the *patronage* whose volunteer members devoted themselves—thus assisting the state and the courts—to such precarious groups as abandoned children, discharged prisoners and aliens, and categories of the insane. I saw an example here of civic intervention in keeping with democratic goals. Deschamps was always looking up one of his "cases." I cite this meeting as an example of the best kind of European influence which diffused itself at many levels among France's Allies from the New World who were too often unfamiliar with its precious cultural and political legacies.

Like Louvain, Tournai was again damaged in World War II and Deschamps' faithful historical restoration was again called for.

My impromptu journal as well as the letters were written out of the action going on, history in the making, as experienced by one of the nameless participants in the ranks. In this light one may hear in them the voice of actuality—the rich registers of human transactions—often forfeited by more formal rehearsal. It is my hope that something of this original context and its often missing overtones may here have been recovered.

At the end of my initial months in the Paris Service, my enlistment in the ambulance corps as anticipated took me in February to Section 2 of the Field Service in the Argonne. In June a six-month stint with Section 3 in Macedonia followed, all this leading to my enlistment as a private in the U.S. Field Artillery in November, 1917, one year after my first arrival in Paris. I will preface the extended account of my service with Section 3, with details of my initiation at the front in the Field Service with Section 2.

This section was then not far west of Verdun during a relatively quiet spell, evacuating casualities of its French division from dug-out dressing-stations in the forested hills of the Argonne. These posts, with their doctors and stretcher-bearers, were linked with the maze of trenches extending through a belt of pulverized forest, a calcined and inhuman landscape which was the result of two years of bombardment. Our evacuations, often in the dark and without the use of our headlights, were impeded by snow. Since at that time there was no antifreeze for the radiators, at night we had to turn on our motors from time to time to prevent freezing.

Section 2 had long been noted for its experienced *chefs* [group leaders] and colorful drivers. When I joined it I found a dozen exceptional Harvard men of the classes of 1917–1919.

I remember the day on which we saw the official French announcement of America's declaration of war on an *affiche* at nearby Ste. Ménéhould, and the euphoria with which this was greeted by the French. We in the Field Service, however, continued with our engagements since it would be a long time before our American Expeditionary Forces could take part in the conflict.

It was with my enlistment and experiences in the U.S. Artillery that my memoir, my journal and letters, take on a special interest since they now link up with the more critical phases of the war and document many of its aspects at this grass-roots and ingenuous level. Routine transactions come into view in their specificity, and momentous ones take on a new dimension as sensed in the ranks. Especially valuable here in this transcription is the resulting portrayal of the American combatants with their undeniable commitments but also their betrayals and confusions.

My absence from my battery during September and October 1918, when I was hospitalized and detained in various camps and quarantine, meant that I saw many aspects of the war—and of France in the war—apart from my months at the front. My notes on these periods, therefore, have their relevance. My rehearsal properly ends with a full-dress account of the shattering attack by our division and others on November 1, 1918, which led in a few days to the Armistice.

For less immediate but early transcription of aspects of the War, I have occasionally cited my *Battle-Retrospect and Other Poems*, published in 1923 by Yale University Press in the Yale Series of Younger Poets. The only earlier use of this journal was in a chapter in George Panichas' symposium on World War I—*Promise of Greatness: The War of 1914–1918* (New York: John Day, 1968). This chapter was entitled "At the Nethermost Piers of History: World War I, A View from the Ranks."

I would like to highlight here some specific ideas about history in connection with this book. I am concerned that readers may misjudge my motives in writing either my original journal at the time of the war or its current presentation in which successive layers of retrospect or reflection may have been added. When I began what I at first called my War Diary I did not think of it in terms of an eventual historical source or documentation. These private notations, in view of their long disregard, might rather have taken on the character of a "time capsule" except that their form indicated no such pretension. Actually, however, their very informality and unprogrammed nature conveyed important aspects of what was transpiring.

Such deeper nuances of our experience were reinforced when, more recently in the process of editing, the original journal was exposed to new and related clusters of reportage, anecdote, and reflection. This melding of old and new has resulted in the present writing: a many-layered memoir or interwoven mosaic, full of echoes and resonances of the original experience.

What especially has troubled me is that, given my divinity school connections and my professional identification with studies in biblical literature, readers might fail to recognize my primary motivation in this book as that of historian. If other cultural soundings enter into my rehearsal they are in the interest of a fuller historical understanding. If my interest theologically is in Armageddon, this focus on Alpha and Omega properly includes all wisdoms in its survey.

Any historical representation which aims to be searching must recognize certain criteria of adequacy to the total givens of the human story, and many histories forego these essential dimensions in their portrayals. Thus human experience and the import of happenings are deeply determined by imaginative and mythical factors and their importance is often forfeited by pragmatic and schematized versions of events. The density and personal particularity of war experience, for example, call for the gifts of poet and novelist.

I recurrently introduce observations into my reminiscences which occur to me at this much later time of their transcription. This melding of past and present, these correspondences of now remote with our contemporary situation, like a triangulation, may well illuminate the original record and experience.

For an example of this continuity through change I cite news reports of the war in the Persian Gulf as I write (February 1991). Batteries of the Second American Marine Division are engaged in firing missions against the Iraqis on the border of Kuwait. This division, "The Indian

Head," is the same reconstituted one whose first deployment in war I have been recalling. Its identity through World War II and a long period of preeminent service in Korea has been maintained. In World War I it was the only division which included Marine regiments, and for a time its commander was the Marine General John Archer Lejeune. One reason its identity has been so jealously preserved is because of the pride of this Corps in the exploits of its Marines especially in the Château-Thierry and Belleau Wood theater of action.

The press accounts indicate that its artillery still includes 155mm howitzers, the same caliber as those of our A Battery of 1918, but also more powerful 203mm howitzers. Today they are of course motorized. The gunners also have more sophisticated instruments for targeting and night firing.

It would be another matter to ask about the continuity of motivations in this later American involvement. This vexed issue would, however, point to similar agonizing differences as to the urgencies and scope of America's role in the tangled cause of international order and security.

Another topical matter which impinges on my reminiscences is current publication dealing with the Great War. Despite the now severe limitations on my reading I am aware especially of the continuing interest in the British poets and writers whose testimony to the war was so widely appreciated in the years of disenchantment which followed it. What is curious, however, about this vogue is that the books in question are not really about the war itself but about its afterimage, its legend and its literary-cultural aspects. These biographies or psychographs of Julian Grenfell, Wilfred Owen, and Edmund Blunden, this continuing attention to the recitals of Robert Graves, Siegfried Sassoon, Ford Madox Ford, among others, reflects a postwar preoccupation.

This skirting of the war itself and what it was about is well illustrated by the very title and theme of a 1990 volume entitled *A War Imagined: The First World War and English Culture*, by Samuel Hynes. According to the reviewer for the *Times Literary Supplement*, Mick Imlah, Hynes sees the war in these writings as a myth imagined by these and other combatants in retrospect in lieu of the actuality, the meaninglessness, the incoherence of their experience. The author cites participants for whom the years of war were as a term in chaos, a "gap in history." The surviving fabulists compensated themselves by their myth of disenchantment, their disabusement with "the Old Men," "The Big Words," Parades, and any supposed "Turning Point" toward a better future.

Hynes supplies . . . instances of writers silenced by the indescribable: Ford Madox Ford (Hueffer), for example, overlooking "the most amazing fact of history," whose dilemma Hynes sees as an archetypal failure of imagination: "Part of it, like the territory that he saw from his hilltop, might be described . . . but the war itself could not be *imagined*. For to imagine it would be to discover its significance; and as Hueffer looked down at it 'it all seemed to signify nothing.' " [3]

The reviewer notes that the title of this work recalls Paul Fussell's "classic," *The Great War and Modern Memory.* Fussell's *Killing in Verse and Prose and Other Essays*, which also deals with the war, is reviewed in this same issue of *TLS.* My question to such cultural historians concerned with the aftermath of the war is the following: Should they not, precisely as historians, despite the bafflement of their witnesses, trace the links and deeper continuities which ran through the war and into that sequel with which they are concerned? * In their capitulation to what they see as enigma and meaninglessness, they identify and vindicate "modern" mood and outlook which neglects more fundamental and enduring motivations and perspectives as they operated even in the maelstrom of the war. Sententious as it may sound, wisdom like a cable runs through changing times and climates of opinion.

Another neglected factor which operates in our experience and representation of history is the context of expectation, intentionality, the constraints of the past and the claims of the future, which condition all choices and action. If one envisages the moral factors in history, account should be taken of all such basic and contributory orientations.

*Amos Wilder incorrectly identifies Samuel Hynes and Paul Fussell as historians. Both are literary scholars, although Fussell is now identified with broader cultural commentary. Because of advanced blindness during the last decade of his life, Wilder's scholarly reading was largely restricted to reviews read with the aid of a machine that greatly magnified the text.

17

*

Prologue

In my unprogrammed narrative I do not, of course, list and identify such basic elements, but the reader will note certain relevant and recurring emphases or motifs which call for the wider sensitivity.

My focus on the "view from the ranks" opens the perspective to a generalized perception prior to that of any code or indoctrination. By thus directing attention to the common and anonymous soldier one is more aware of universal and immemorial aspects of his role and its parameters. In the same way, our classics about Everyman tell us things about the individual which would otherwise be lost to sight. My journal as "a view from the ranks" may well therefore be transparent on aspects of war which take us back to archaic antecedents and thus enrich the picture.

However rude and fragmentary my narrative often is, there may be some important compensation in its insistence on being at the heart of the action itself. Of course it is the very nature of such a journal to be present at the episodes recounted. But I make much of the dramatic sense of being a participant in the unfolding of events. One will note more than one occasion when I speak of "the overwhelming sense of history in the making" and of "awe toward the future." These expressions were prompted especially by the prodigious barrages incident to our great attacks. But our participation in the more common routines of duty was animated by a constant sense of fatefulness and excitement which related to the stakes and import of the war. This, indeed, was also the reason why I could characterize my journal as "at the nethermost piers of history."

What I had in mind here was a quasi-geological sense of being at the exposed center of the seismic forces—the shifting tectonic plates of the historical process—and their unpredictable outcomes. In more familiar terms, I would understand our ordeal historically as that of those fatefully involved in the millennial vicissitudes of our European vocation to civil order and fulfillment. As this mission engaged the original powers of darkness and chaos, one could understand the veritable paroxysms of evil and the transcendent redemptive initiatives incident to the confrontation. In this light such earlier analogies as those of Apocalypse and Armageddon seem profoundly relevant.

＊　＊　＊

Part One

With the American Field
Service in Macedonia

The following retrospect on one of the lesser known the-
atres of the Great War rests in large part on a journal written at the time.
From the time I went to France in 1916 until my return in 1919 I kept
a journal in the small black *carnets*, measuring seven inches by four,
familiar to French children. This record is amplified with letters home
and with later observations, both historical and personal, all with a view
to evoking the experience of many young Americans who served with the
French in the Field Service before the United States entered the war.

After such a lapse of time an old diary, like old letters, may have
a particular interest, especially if the notations are linked with public
events of some importance. Such extempore jottings, even of a minor
actor in a marginal scene, retain something of their original actuality.
Some buried layer of the past, moments otherwise sunk in oblivion, are
suddenly recaptured as when a time capsule is opened.

After more than seventy years, my interest, however, extends beyond
personal sentiment or exotic rehearsal. Our newer generations can well
be alerted to a past which extends back beyond Vietnam and World

War II. Those of us who served in the Great War often feel baffled by the hazy unreality it has assumed in the popular mind and the simplifications with which it is reported. Though all wars have mythical overtones and in the sequel take on features both of fable and cliché, these all go back finally to the very human particularities of history and to the actualities of events and persons. The youth of today, for example, may well be reminded that their grandfathers, whose portraits they have seen in the olive drab uniforms of World War I doughboys, were not tin soldiers or cutouts from some cyclorama but actual youths like themselves with their own ideas and values, their own ardors and dismays.

By the late summer of 1917 two of the Field Service ambulance sections had now for some time been serving in the Balkans. As an elite corps of many of the most adventurous of that college generation the Field Service took on a glamorous character, second only to the Lafayette Escadrille. Its volunteer aspect, the sense of fraternity in high emprise, the resourcefulness, talents, verve, and ribald humor in the section, the comradeship-in-arms with the French personnel in underground dressing stations and *poste de secours*—all this evoked older images of chivalry. Like many college students at that time my interest in ambulance service in France had been quickened by fellow students at Yale who had returned to school after a period of service. After the winter of 1916–1917 in Paris I joined Section 2 on the edge of the Argonne.[1]

> *June 16, 1917.* At breakfast the General [our section Chef at the time, Francis D. Ogilvie, an Englishman from Sussex who had been with the Service since its origins in 1914] asked if any of us wanted to go to Salonika, having rec'd a telegram from Andrew [A. Piatt Andrew, Inspector General of the AFS, in Paris] asking for the names of volunteers to go to Salonika, on the basis of a six months engagement beginning July 1st. After 30 minutes of perspiration and absolute deadlock, I walked down and told him I had decided to go. An immediate answer and a final one was required thus in no time at all . . . I trembled all morning.

Among the stray items copied into the back of this *carnet* of my journal is the following quatrain from La Fontaine's *Fables* extolling blind venture.

Fortune aveugle suit aveugle hardiesse.

Le sage quelquefois fait bien d'exécuter

Avant que de donner le temps à la sagesse

D'envisager le fait, et sans la consulter.[2]

No doubt a chief factor in my decision was the lure of the East and of Biblical lands. The main reason for hesitation was that this new six-month engagement might postpone enlistment in the American Expeditionary Forces when they arrived. Those of us who had joined the Ambulance Service in 1916 had doubted whether the United States would ever enter the war. When war was declared in April 1917 many of us wished to transfer to combatant service in the American army without having to return to the States.

As it turned out, however, my Macedonian assignment did not delay this opportunity. When the AEF arrived in force in the fall of 1917 it took over the Field Service. But because the United States had not declared war on Bulgaria, Sections 3 and 10 in the Balkans were turned over to the French and those of us in these sections were free to enlist in one or another branch of the American army.

The days that I was in Paris awaiting our departure for the Balkans were marked by one momentous occasion.

Paris, July 4. Miss [Blanche] Stanley and I took a taxi to the Picpus Cemetery and stood in the crowd while Gen'l Pershing, Gen'l Joffre, Ambassador Sharpe, Minister of War Painlevé, and others walked right by us. Miss Stanley introduced me to Col. Stanton who was one of the speakers at these exercises incident to wreathing Lafayette's grave. All preceded by the marching of the 2nd Battalion [16th Infantry?] thru the crowded thoroughfares of Paris amid wild enthusiasm. A greater day I never saw.

Blanche Stanley was an American painter living in Paris, daughter and sister of senior American officers and hostess of many Americans in uniform in her studio from the earliest days. She was happiest when she was literally wrestling lonely American boys on leave in Paris from the clutches of the *cocottes* at the place St.-Germain outside its famous cafés.

What is interesting about my on-the-spot notation is that I had some-how missed Stanton's famous words, "Lafayette, we are here!" Knowing of them later I long shared the widely held view that Pershing himself had pronounced them. I have often cited this as an example of the fal-libility of eyewitness report.* Indeed, accounts of the episode by later historians, both French and American, vary a great deal. Pershing in his memoirs says that he had asked Stanton to speak for him, though Painlevé had induced Pershing to add a few remarks.

From its beginnings, the Field Service with its motto, "Friends of France," was deeply animated by historical Franco-American senti-ment. Many today will put this down to the naiveté with which our generation envisaged the war. Our later disabused wisdom discounts all such historical mythology together with other prewar idealizations of patriotism and sacrifice, supposedly unmasked as rhetoric and propa-ganda in the sequel. No doubt our ardors were inflated and naive. But another kind of wisdom will recognize that all such idealisms are mixed. Illusion and insight, fable and reality, go hand in hand.

The Francophilia of the Field Service no doubt had its romantic as-pects. When Pershing arrived in Paris both the current Marquis de Lafayette and Comte de Rochambeau hailed him. For my part I find a warrant for our sentiment in the actual France of the war years. The France which we imagined from school days, with whatever romanti-cism, was compounded of that Roman republican order so much ad-mired by Thomas Jefferson and the Christian model of Saint Louis and Joan of Arc. But this France was not a figment in 1917. Though our American volunteers would not have known his name, the poet Charles Péguy, who died in the Battle of the Marne in 1914, had incarnated both legacies in peacetime and in arms. His role was more revelatory for his people in its disarray and ordeal than that of such patriots as Maurice Barrès or such pacifists as Romain Rolland, admirable as they were. And those fealties which Péguy and others represented we our-selves encountered in our associations with the nameless men clad in

*See Amos N. Wilder, "Between Reminiscence and History: A Miscellany," *Proceedings of the Massachusetts Historical Society* 87 (1975), pp. 105–117.

horizon blue with whom we performed our tasks or whom we carried in
our ambulances.

After reporting to our Field Service administration in Paris for this
new assignment I found that quite a large number of us were slated for
the long journey to Salonika and service in General Maurice Sarrail's
Army of the Orient. Replacements were due in my own Section 3 in
Macedonia, and almost all the drivers in Section 10 in Albania were to
be replaced. An entry in my journal on the day of our departure reads
as follows:

> *Paris, July 7.* 25 of Section 10 and 11 of Section 3 had early
> breakfast at Rue Raynouard [headquarters of the AFS in Passy],
> and left the Gare de Lyons at 7:45.

Thus began our long trip to Macedonia: first by civilian train to Marseilles; then by troop train via Leghorn and Rome to Tarentum; then by
troop ship around Greece to Salonika; and finally by troop train again
to the neighborhood of Monastir (modern day Bitola) and the Serbian
front. Replacements to Section 10 went on to Koritza in Albania. These
were Stanford University men, almost all of whom had just arrived from
California as a section, and who were willing to be diverted to the Balkan front despite their already lengthy journey.

It was my brother, Thornton, who was most envious and eloquent
when he heard of my crusade toward the East. He was working that summer on the Berea College farm in Kentucky just before his transfer to
Yale from Oberlin. He had in the meantime seen a picture of Section 3
in the *Saturday Evening Post* accompanying an account of the Field Service by John Masefield, and he thought he recognized me in the group.

> When mother wrote me that you like Richard the Lion Hearted had
> set your face toward the Levant . . . and that your address read Sec-
> tion SSU-3, I shipped the picture to her or lost it. . . . O notable
> Crusader, did not Richard also wear a crimson cross when he went
> among the Saracens? And did not he too embark at Massiglia? Per-
> chance he too touched at Salonika . . . O that my hair were blown

by an Aegean wind or that beneath my feet the prow folded the "holy waters of Pauline memory." Instead I drag my hoe over sod that only the tradition of Daniel Boone enriches, and that but doubtfully.

It is true that our ambulances exhibited a large Red Cross as evidence of our non-belligerent status. It is also true that we went among the Saracens in the sense that Islam was well represented in southern Serbia with its mosques and minarets. It is also true that it was at Massiglia/

Marseilles that we left the civilian world behind and joined a troop train, though we actually embarked at Tarentum. As for "the holy waters of Pauline memory," I have so much confidence in Thornton's citations that I am sure it must come from Dante or another classic.

During our journey to the front I wrote to Thornton of our passage through the Riviera:

> *July 10.* The train is just starting out of Nice . . . We left this morning at 1 A.M. from Marseilles. In the black freight yard we loaded 3 big drays of our baggage into a freight car. Then we saw 1,000 troops [including Senegalese] loaded beneath the arc-lights. They were put 32 in a freight car, with a four-day trip in hot weather ahead. We were put 8 to a 2nd class compartment (39 altogether). In ours we have us 4 Oberlin fellows, Lumen Tenney, Waller Harrison, and Jimmie Todd. [Thornton and I had both known these men at Oberlin.]
> At Cannes the train stopped 3 ½ hours within 75 feet of the blue waves . . . Into the water we all went, naked, and such a swim as never before.

> *Livorno, July 12.* We slept [on the train] as prostrate as possible-two of the fellows above in the satchel racks, and the rest of us stretched cross the seats and baggage between.

Memories surface of occasions not reported in my journal: glimpses of the white bluffs of Carrara, the leaning tower of Pisa. At Rome during a short stop members of the American colony rushed us about a few sites. In retrospect I cannot but think, ironically, of this caged transit through the length of storied Italy and the fabled Mediterranean. This was a different kind of "grand tour." The itineraries, maps, and landscapes of the soldier belong to a world apart. This came home to me most vividly on our return from Macedonia later when we were transported to Itia on the Gulf of Corinth, and I later learned that we had passed close to Parnassus and Delphi without knowing it.

Embarking at Tarentum we were part of a convoy which traveled only at night. My journal tells of the maneuvering of our unlighted ships to avoid enemy submarines and movements in single file through suspected mine fields. Our successive anchorages were off Corfu, Navarin (Pylos), Milos, and Skyros. From Skyros English destroyers took us to Salonika, which we reached on July 22.

With its ancient churches, mosques, synagogues, walls, and cemeteries and its modern cafés, emporia, and bazaars, Salonika was a palimpsest of history and the Levant. What immediately struck us in the throngs was the diversity of uniforms of the various armies operating in this theatre: French, British, Serb, Italian, Russian, Greek. No less disparate was the kaleidoscope of the traits and garbs of the population. The city rose from the long sweep of the Aegean with its busy shipping and the belt of commerce, banking, and diversion which parallel it, through the ancient enclaves of the various faiths and communities, to a veritable jungle and catacomb of tenements, caves, and huts below the medieval wall which circled the seaport on the hill above. Beyond were the tented encampments, white and ghostlike, of both troops and refugees.

The city as we saw it is well evoked in *The Handbook of Macedonia*, compiled by the Naval Intelligence Division of the British Admiralty and published in 1920.

> Salonika, the metropolis of the Balkans, is a Babel of races, languages, beliefs, customs, ideas and aspirations, in which Semites, Mongols, Pelasgians, Slavs and Teutons are confounded. The street vendors talk Turkish, Spanish, French, Greek and Italian with equal fluency. Spanish is the prevalent language of the slums; that of large business transactions, the big shops and the fashionable cafés is French; ordinary shopping is carried on in Bulgarian, Turkish or Greek. The boatmen swear in English and Italian, the cab drivers in Turkish and Spanish.[3]

The *Handbook* notes that the population in 1914 was 170,000. Of these 56 percent were Jewish; 18 percent Greek; 9 percent Moslem plus 11 percent representing a Jewish sect which spoke Turkish and professed a reformed Islam. There were also Serbs, Armenians, Catholic foreigners, and Bulgarians.

To return to my own notations of July 23–24:

There are Turks, sprawled in Jovian serenity among their draperies, there are priests of unknown gods, cabalistic worshipers and spiritualists, Mohamadan mosques, Jewish synogogues, non-conformist huts, a French primary school; boot-blacks, cigarette sellers and little girls with dime novels who go among the tables at the cafes; a moving picture show where they give the "the Clutching Hand" under the title "Mysteries of New York" . . . There is one great store here, the town's Wanamaker, advertised on all the street cars— "Steins"—on the door of which is the notice "This store is out of bounds for members of the allied armies."

I had lunch with Dr. Ryan [decorated career Red Cross official who had served in Serbia before the war]. He answered my questions about the best methods of arranging for the Balkans after the war by recommending that the whole district be covered 50 feet deep with water till all life was extinct.

I read on the history of Salonika this afternoon [*La Ville Convoitée —Salonique* by P. Risel (1917) and *Pro Macedoine* by Victor Berard (1904)]. Then walked up to the wall at the top of the hill. I went thru some 2 miles of not streets but gutters or sewers, bordered by ancient stone huts, a labyrinth; filled with children with shining faces, with old women with faces like gray stones. In between were all the gradations in the gradual dimming and suffocation of the life-spirit . . . The women and children were fetching water. The men were down at the Port carrying these tremendous loads on their backs.

I followed the wall—a great crenelated mass—up to the citadel —and then turned down. I passed where the Forum and the Hippodrome and the Stadium used to be. There is a great variety of ancient cemeteries. I saw part of a funeral procession go by—of a poor family. At the end were two women, one helping the other who was in a terrible state of despair and cried fearfully. When they came to the gate of the cemetery she became quite distracted and could not bear to go in . . . Such cries must shrivel up soul and body.

My journal recalls Paul's visit to Thessalonika. He had spent at least three weeks in this "free city" of the Empire, probably in the winter of A.D. 49–50 in the course of that journey which first took him beyond Asia Minor; a visit described in the seventeenth chapter of the Acts of the Apostles and vividly evoked in 1 Thessalonians written soon afterwards. When we went west toward Monastir we were roughly following Rome's great artery, the Via Egnatia, along which Paul had come to Macedonia from Troas.

In Salonika, this Levantine metropolis of many faiths, in which epochs of Mediterranean history seemed to live on, a bottomless well of the past, one felt that one could more easily picture Paul's own theatre and mission. In particular it seemed easier to recognize the obstacles which confronted the new faith, and the seeming hopelessness of any such new impulse as the one which Paul introduced into the welter of history. In modern Salonika as in that of Paul one could recognize the sway of millennial folkways, the impasse and stagnation of ancient habits, foreclosing any such new horizon as the one Paul evoked. The scandal of that thrust is reflected in the charge made against him by his opponents in the city: "These men who have turned the world upside down have come here also" (Acts 17:6). Evidence of that impact was, however, visibly manifest to us especially in the great church of St. Demetrius, often compared to the resplendent Hagia Sophia in Constantinople. Before we returned in October 1917 the church had been reduced to a hollow shell by the great fire that swept over a large part of the city on August 18, 1917.

The last leg of our journey took us west about a hundred miles by supply train to the neighborhood of Monastir. To our surprise Section 3 was now attached to the Second Serbian Division and stationed high up in a mountainous area east of that city. Four of the Serbian cars finally located us after dark at the railhead, Sakulevo, to which we had returned after detraining farther on. They then took us by dizzy ascents, an hour and a half drive, to our station at Slivika in this savage terrain overlooking the Tserna River and the lines. This stretch of the front had been established only a few months earlier when Austrians and Bulgarians had been driven out of these heights by a Serbian action which had already become legendary in the war under the name "The Rock of Blood."*

Centuries of Turkish control of the area ended when they were driven out in the Balkan Wars of 1912–1913, at which time western Macedonia was divided between Greece and Serbia by the Treaty of Bucharest. In 1914 the Serbians at first withstood Austria's attack. But in 1915 Bulgaria sided with the Central Powers, induced by promises of territorial expansion in the area. The Serbian army was then overwhelmed and driven south into Albania and to the Adriatic by armies commanded by the German general von Mackensen. At the same time the Gallipoli campaign of the British became hopeless once the Central Powers could reinforce the Turks through Bulgaria.

In the autumn of 1916 the French divisions near Monastir and in the mountains to the west realized that they could use the Ford ambulances which had proved so effective in the same kind of terrain on the home front. Consequently, Section 3 (originally organized in Paris in April 1915) which had served on the heights of Alsace, was sent to Macedonia in October 1916. Our colleagues had arrived in the immediate sequel of the push which had driven the enemy north of the Greek frontier to the heights above Monastir. An account of their activities in the *History of the American Field Service* includes the following:

In November [1916] the Section was assigned to the Monastir sector. Several times cars were detached and sent over into the wild mountainous country of Albania to serve French troops there, and on one occasion the Section was sent to Greece with a French force ordered to maintain Greek neutrality.[4]

Section 10 had also gone to the Balkans, arriving in Salonika in January 1917. There its cars and equipment were assembled, and it left in

---

*The Rock of Blood refers to a bloody moment in the widely heralded victory of Serbian troops over the Bulgarians in 1916.

convoy for the Albanian front, taking up quarters in the town of Koritza. In this area the terrain was even more difficult. On a steep hill near Lake Ostrava the French stationed a dozen *poilus* to help push the cars over a grade. This Section included two of my former Thacher School friends, Kimberly Stuart from M.I.T. and Philip Newbold Rhinelander from Harvard, both of whom later joined the American aviation, Rhinelander losing his life in that service.

But in 1917, in order to limit the enemy's access to the Mediterranean and to secure the neutrality of Greece, a French and British force under General Sarrail, which included elements withdrawn from the Dardanelles, established a fortified camp in and west of Salonika. In 1916 the Allies manned a line running from Albania in the west to the Aegean. The Serbs had been re-equipped by the French. The British held the front east of the Vardar into Thrace. In addition to Italians there were ten thousand Russians, who after the revolution in 1917 became disaffected. On June 29, shortly before our arrival, the Greeks joined the Allies. King Constantine, whose wife was a sister of the German Kaiser, was deposed in favor of his son, Alexander, and Venizélos returned to power as prime minister.

In early 1917 the Allies in this theatre numbered 600,000 in all. One authority reports 210,000 French, 180,000 British, 152,000 Serbs, besides others. Many, however, were incapacitated, especially by malaria. In the official volumes on British military operations in Macedonia, in connection with the measures taken against malaria we read that the troops were supplied with quinine, netting, sleeping nets, and masks. A photograph captioned "Quinine Parade" shows a squad lined up for administration of spoonfuls of quinine.

During the war and later there were those among the Allies who questioned the wisdom of the Salonika operations and considered them a "useless dispersion of troops which might have been more usefully employed elsewhere." The expedition showed no tangible result for three years. It required shipping when shipping and tonnage were scarce, and when submarines made all such traffic dangerous. Over half a million troops were involved, and the Germans called it "their largest concentration camp, an enemy army prisoner of itself."[5]

Although the French and British had not been able to save the Serbs in 1915, they prevented the Central Powers from taking Salonika and from bringing Greece into the war on their side until 1918. The Allies thus kept them from establishing new submarine bases and controlling the eastern Mediterranean, including Egypt and the Suez Canal. Britain's connection with India and Australia was better safeguarded. Furthermore, an army of 750,000 Bulgarians and Austrians was tied down for the duration.

It was on this front that the Central Powers first gave way in disastrous fashion in September 1918. The offensive of the Allies, which was commanded by General Franchet d'Esperey, began just east of Monastir at the bend of the Tserna River. It led to a complete collapse of the Bulgarians and the country's withdrawal from the war, which hastened the German capitulation in the west.

The population of the Monastir area in western Macedonia was a mixture of all the long-feuding nationalities and faiths of the region, along with a surviving peasant stock of Vlacks (Wallachians), as well as settled gypsies. Monastir had numerous minarets, but the people were mainly Christian, their various Orthodox rites traditionally linked with Constantinople. Rebecca West's remarkable *Black Lamb and Grey Falcon: Record of a Journey Through Jugoslavia* (1941), has a moving account of the Greek Orthodox liturgy of the peasants in whose communion cup she sees "the last drops of the Byzantine tradition."

It is an old story that the ordeals of the armies on the Western front in the Great War could take on mythical overtones. In David Jones' *In Parenthesis* and in such novels as Montherlant's *Songe* and Faulkner's *Fable*, the centuries collapse and the scenes and actions evoke ancient prototypes from the annals of Greece and Rome. The casqued men on the Somme or before Verdun merge with those who served at Waterloo under Napoleon or at Lake Regulus or Thermopylae. Something like this colored our experience even in the less dramatic vicissitudes of our service. In this exotic theatre in which our Western forces were immersed in a timeless Levant we could sometimes feel ourselves actors in an historical script, our parts determined by ancient scenarios.

Travelers speak of the spell or the magic of faraway places, but for those of us involved in the ongoing vicissitudes and pageant of Macedonia this spell could be even more compelling. We were not merely observers of the picturesque and the antique. We were caught up as participants in the cyclical fates of the region: the features of the land, the valleys and watercourses; the ancient habitations and their immemorial ways and tracks, fords, and bridges; the economies of tillage and market-place. These continuities were the stage of our action as of earlier annals of war here in times both recent and remote. Thus the very geography of our routine duties was haunted by older feuds and campaigns, and their bands and phalanxes and legions.

The imagination of the soldier lends itself to this kind of surrealism, is vulnerable to such visitations. Displaced from his civilian existence and its freedom of action, he is subject both to a regimen of authority and to overruling and unpredictable historical forces. His lot is one of fate and fortune in the wider prospect, and one of hazard and luck more immediately. The world of war has its own time and space, recognized most vividly by soldiers on leave when they move back to the lines from the boulevards and music halls of Paris or London, resuming their helmets and gas masks.

I have noted that the maps and charts of military operations are different from those of peacetime. War establishes its own frontiers, capitals, junctions, and networks. One need only think of the prestige of such names as Verdun, the Marne, Belleau Wood, or Chemin des Dames, the Ypres Salient, Hill 304, or the Bar-le-Duc road. Even after the war when veterans revisit the battle zones they find themselves moving through a different constellation than that of their road map. In view of this intense perception it is not surprising that our experience even in our quieter theatre had similar overtones. But it is important to distinguish this inevitable heightening of our reactions from the romanticizing of war, which was for the most part confined to the civilian world.

At Slivika, then—to return to my journal—we had reached the front. As in all theatres, approach to the front "concentrates the mind wonderfully" and leads to a quickening of the pulse and all vibrations and reflexes. Whether in France or the Balkans the front included not only the frontline trenches but the related network of communicating trench systems, roads hidden and exposed, battery emplacements, observation posts, advanced supply depots, and so on. Our ambulance station was near the outer edge of this zone but within the area of occasional shelling and hostile airplane surveillance. Not far was the perimeter within which at night all vehicles extinguished their lights.

What was peculiar about our sector was that the units we were serving were so far below us. When we descended the gorge we found the Serbian casualties and *malades* "in a series of little arbors where they lay on the ground under a roof of branches." The wounded were attended by a medical officer and *brancardiers* (stretcher-bearers), who always served us tea or Turkish coffee before we set out on our evacuation trip, which I noted as "Serbian appreciation of American relief work!" Returning with our loads we passed our mountain station and took them down again to a hospital well in the rear.

Slivika, July 28. [The morning after our midnight arrival.] When I awoke I saw that the knoll we were on dropped away on three sides to a deep valley, while on the other side the road mounts and mounts by dusty and dizzy zig-zags up over the mountain, and thence over several more still higher—as I found when I went up with Lovering Hill, the Chef [Harvard '10 from New York City] and Lowry [Thomas Lowry, non-college driver from Royal Oak, Michigan] for our driving tests. Way out here, 1,000 miles from nowhere, we passed camion after camion going and coming— driven by the British mostly—roaring up in low gear, mile after mile. We went up for a good half hour—low gear almost every foot of the way, and we didn't go to the top and we'd started half-way up only—Hill says the grades are worse yet in the Vosges, tho' the roads are better. We came down in low gear as well. From where we went we could see the summit of mount Vetternick to the East ["The Rock of Blood"]. To the North-West the location of the trenches was visible . . . 15 or more miles off. Below us were two great Red Crosses marked on the ground [our own Slivika encampment].

The Serbs have put up a green thatch roof shelter where we eat

and it is like picnicking. There are also sheds, made of thatch
or the tin from gas cans, for the Lieut [our French Officer, Lt.
Derode], for the kitchen etc . . . At 11:00 we had hors d'oeuvre of
canned salmon—a fine roast, with cabbage and boiled potatoes,
lots of good butter, canned cherries and coffee.

Slivika, July 30. I was awarded car 334, the wreck of the section,
tho not necessarily a bad car . . . [it] had been carelessly driven by
C—— who in trying to pass another car very soon after he had
got here—racing—had a blow-out and run into the bank, rolling
over a couple of times. He was sent home to Paris the night we got
here for the offense and had not been allowed to drive it in the two
months intervening. The car was pretty well loosened up all over,
and one side well smashed.—but after a couple days work with
Mr. Roberts it is now in fair shape. . . . Among the dramatis per-
sonae of this section are Roberts, the mechanic [George Roberts, a
non-college driver from Boston] and Logan [George Logan, Jr., of
Princeton from Pittsburgh] who were on our Bordeaux-Paris convoy
trip last February. [Twenty of us had driven newly assembled Ford
chassis to Paris at that time.] Logan is the one that having pneumonia rec'd ice-pack treatment for appendicitis on the night we spent
in Chartres—and who last year was taken prisoner and kept at work
by the Bulgars when he was working for some English hospital they
captured.

We had only a week up in our eyrie with the Serbs. My journal tells
of the comic reactions of the new recruits as they returned shaken from
their driving tests with Hill during which they backed and turned around
and changed tires on hairpin turns above these gorges. This was my second driving test in the service. When I joined the Paris Service in Neuilly
in November 1916 I was tested on one of the Buick sixes ambulances
with which that corps was equipped. Because we were stationed at the
Lycée Pasteur, near the Porte Maillot, my examiner chose an obvious
run for my test, none other than the Champs Elysées, which I success-
fully negotiated from the Etoile to the Tuileries.

From Slivika the Section moved on August 3 to a site just south of
Monastir. The next day I wrote home:

Passing down the great gorge of the Tserna we came out on the plain of Monastir [near Sakulevo where we had so recently detrained on arrival]. At 7:45 A.M. after a fast convoy trip we got to this little camp up a ravine [Bistrika], off a road that runs to Monastir. Below us is the wide valley going down to the sea and the Greek frontier. Back of us to the West, the mountains [separating us from Albania]. There is a good sized brook that runs past the camp. On the edge a large square of Ford cars, the repair trucks, the kitchen on wheels, the dining table with benches all in the sun [later under a tent]. Up the north bank half of us live in dugouts that peep out of the hill . . . Others live in one of the section tents on a pretty meadow above the rise on the south bank. I am lucky in that the dugout I got had already had a roof of branches and [tent] cloth. The others have had to work leveling the floors, building up the walls with gasoline cans filled with earth, and roofing with canvas.

This morning I went up to Monastir with Hill and one of the old boys, saw the streets and the field hospital there. Two cars wait there all the time on post [on call] . . . Then there is a 36 kilometer night time run from there back past us to Florina [in Greece] where the base hospitals are . . . The heights above Monastir are lined with enemy trenches and the town is absolutely at their mercy as far as shelling goes. It's only by a sort of laissez-faire that we got back and forth on any of these roads. It's as though you were on Mt. Carmel [outside New Haven where my family lived] with all kinds of guns and took only a languid interest in stopping traffic on Whitney Avenue, or knocking the town to pieces. The Bulgarians bomb and shell the town occasionally and stop men and camions from using the road in daylight, and that's about all.

If Paul had continued westward beyond Salonika and Pella on the Via Egnatia he would have reached Monastir. The city as we knew it lay on both sides of a narrow river, the Dragor, with its quais and stone bridges, at the mouth of a ravine which opened to the northwest. The British Admiralty's *Handbook of Macedonia* numbers the population (before the flight of many into Greece) at 50,000, made up of Serbs, Vlacks, Turks,

Jews, Bulgarians, Albanians, and Greeks. The city had a Greek arch-bishop. Rebecca West mentions fourteen minarets and portrays Mona-stir as "one of the fairest of all cities . . . with aspects of Arabian Nights atmosphere." The whole area was colorful with acacias, irises, poppies, cornflowers, buttercups, daisies, and meadowsweet. The farms, West notes, had porches with vine-clad poles and iron balconies, decorated, as we also observed, with peppers, squashes, and maize.

What was anomalous about this city under sporadic fire was the way in which civilian life continued. Between calls, we drivers on duty at the hospital would saunter into the shops or stop at a café or yogurt stall. It was not unusual in this part of the world to come across a Serb or Greek who had lived in the States. When one of our drivers was about to snap a photo of a picturesque group he was surprised to hear one of them say: "All right, boys, shoot!" One of the most successful snapshots I took with my Brownie camera was of a young woman in her Macedo-nian finery. Rebecca West describes the women's dress as a series of layers: chemise, dress, waistcoat, plastron, veil, embroidery, sequins, and hieratic designs; part wool, part flax. I photographed the woman in the same hospital yard where I had close call with a shell not long after.

The houses and shops were for the most part one story and without cellars. If a shell arrived in a neighboring street the people would dis-appear but could not go underground. Most shells were misses, but ex-ceptions were inevitable, and we drivers had occasional civilian cases. Earlier drivers had found themselves busy with a prolonged gas attack on part of the city.

As was the case earlier in France with Section 2, this was a quiet front with no massive attacks on either side. Yet, as I have said, the zone of the front everywhere casts its spell. Here was the frontier of worlds in collision and the stage on which we moved took on its special lighting. When we drove out of the city at night to the advanced postes to pick up our casualties we could see the star shells over the lines casting their ominous glare over the trenches.

Bistrika, Aug. 5th. Had my first evacuation today—1 *couché* and 3 *assis-malades.*

The *malades* were often malaria cases. "Dysentery" was used loosely for various kinds of colic and diarrhea, sometimes induced by sudden changes of temperature. We were encouraged to wear muslin bands about our midriffs. These were so long it was easiest to spin like a dervish in putting them on, while someone else held the end. Since we often also wore wrapped rather than leather puttees, we could feel that we were well on the way to becoming mummies. From my journal:

There is just room [in my dug-out] for my short bed and a narrow corridor along it where I have a gas box for my washing. . . . my mosquito netting hangs on sticks from the corners of the cot. A shelf for books, photo equipment, spirit lamp and dishes. My pack and clothing under the bed.

Aug. 10th. The 8th and 9th I was on *repos* [reserve]. Today I am one of the two cars that go to Monastir for 24 hour service. The service begins at 6:30 P.M. when we go up to the hospital in the far quarter of the town. The two who have been on duty take loads to Florina, as do a couple of other cars which go up for that purpose— all the evacuations usually being done at that time [after dark]. Well after dark one of our two cars goes West out along the river to a mysterious dark *poste de secour* in an open field. It is here that the *malades* are brought down from the lines by mule-back, some as far as 5 kil[ometers]. This point has the enemy on two sides, north and west. There is never a light. Files of big two-wheeled carts go out into the dark with provisions. There also one sees big straggling groups of Serbian and Musselman farm laborers going out into the fields at night to work, returning before light. The car stays here on duty until one A.M. making what trips in to the hospital are necessary. . . . During the day there are short trips in town or out in other direction. . . . After supper [at the hospital] the cars take loads to Florina 25 kilos away and get back to camp about 11:30.

In the yogurt shops where we went in Monastir when we were off duty, the yogurt was spooned warm out of large urns and served with *confiture* or with sugar if it was to be had. I had learned a lot about yogurt in a course on "National Efficiency" taught at Yale by the celebrated economist Irving Fisher. In the course, which included a section on public health and longevity, we all had to read *The Prolongation of Life* by Elie Metchnikoff which dealt with longevity in the Balkans and the properties of yogurt.

Bistrika, August 16th. [Letter] On 14th I had three trips—100 kilometers in all. Yesterday I was *en repos*, but at 9 o'clock at night Hill routed me out of bed where I was all snug reading, and I replaced a car on duty that had cracked an axle. The fellow I replaced, Varnum [Richard Varnum of Harvard] went with me, driving part of the way, and we took a Greek *couché, blessé*, down to Florina, getting back at 12:30 A.M. Again, the first thing this morning it was down again with some *assis malades* who didn't act at all sick—So you can see we're earning our daily bread.

It may look easy to the poor soldiers stamping along in the glare with their packs, but mile after mile of jar, jar, bump, bump, roar, dust, and worst of all, the hypnotizing strain of driving without lights when the road and parched plain just swim at you silently and you see things—all this gets on your nerves so that you have to stop sometimes, get out and shake yourself, or you will go mad.

Other times it is great fun. Today an officer I gave a lift to with his baggage wanted to tip me—a dollar or more. A *brancardier* who went down with me insisted with tears in his eyes that I have a drink with him.

Here I recall that on another occasion a portly Greek nurse in uniform refused transportation with me unless she could be accompanied by an orderly. She did not feel safe with one of these wild-west Americans. Or perhaps she confused "Americains" with "Moroccains," so fiercely reputed. In any case I have a picture of her seated next to me on our run with the Serbian orderly crowded in next to her, half on the running board.

August 17th. [Journal] This afternoon the Bulgars began to shell Monastir fairly heavily—worse than since last March—(it is still going on). We can see 5 separate fires in town thru the heavy smoke from our hill 4 miles away. Jack D'Este [Harvard, '10, from Salem, Massachusetts, now Chef of the Section after the departure of Lovering Hill] and Lt. Derode went up, but so far only one or two cars have been called up.

The shelling went on until midnight. East of the Grande Rue the city was practically destroyed. The French military authorities estimated that two thousand shells had fallen between four and eight o'clock that evening. Details of the scene and the panic and sufferings of the population are recorded in a section of the *History of the American Field Service*, written by our fellow driver Charles Amsden (from Harvard and Farmington, New Mexico) who went up to Monastir that evening. Meanwhile, Gilbert Sinclair (University of Minnesota) and Scott Russell (a non-college driver from Chicago) had been on duty during the day. A letter home of August 19 evokes the onset of the bombing as the ridiculous turned into the calamitous. Sinclair and Russell were passing time in a stroll between calls.

> Russ said that he saw the funniest thing in his life when he saw a lot of naked kids, at the first shell, spring from the river, take their clothes under their arms, and fly stark naked down the main street. Gil said he wouldn't have missed it for anything, but when the shells began to come in 18 to the minute for a while he thought it was the end of the world.

In leaving the city later in the day,

> Russ had to detour from the *Grande Rue*—more or less a wall of flame—and got caught in such a hail-storm of "hate" that the load and driver took refuge behind a wall till it passed to another part of town.

I had made a trip the night before the disaster and returned to camp so ill with diarrhea that I was on my back all that day. (A bout of this local ailment took my Oberlin friend Harrison to a hospital for ten days.) The next day I was on duty again. Pieces from my journal tell part of the story.

Saturday, August 18th. The shelling of Monastir proved quite serious. I went up later in the day and saw great patches of ruins to the right of the main road [*Grande Rue*]. Along this street small fires burn still. Varnum and I were on duty at the Hospital after supper. We tossed and I drew *poste*. First I picked up 2 *poilus* too sick to tramp any further at the edge of town. Then 5 *assis* on 1st trip in from *Grand Rocher*. *Medicin-chef* sent me with a guide on a twice-repeated wild goose chase for a sick officer "somewhere about 'Kil. 23'" on the Florina road. He or his attendants were supposed to signal us. . . . We didn't see anything but scared mules and stars, and had to go in low gear all the time. I was dead tired when we returned from the 2nd trip at 1:30 A.M. In the morning we heard that the officer had been picked up by a passing ambulance.

Monastir, August 19th. In the morning Varnum and I had some hot milk with bread at a Turkish shop, the first real milk in ages, then looked at some of the ruins of the bombardment. . . . At 3 I took a great load of surgical supplies 28 kilometers to Gradesnika, [and returned] too late for supper, but got some sardines and yogurt. Left empty at 7 and picked up a number of refugees with their heavy loads for five kilometers.

August 21st. In the ten days, Aug. 11–20, I made 13 separate trips [according to my ten-day report card] carrying 23 *assis* and 7 *couchés*—a total of 407 kilometers, going and coming.

Mail from home, including parcels, reached us dependably. (One letter with blurred address and a surcharge, stamped "Accident de mer"—indicating a torpedoing—reached me later in France.) The army, of course, like a great enclave in the body politic, has its own postal service. We were addressed through a French military bureau in Marseilles, thus "SSU 3, Convois autos, Armée d'Orient, par BCM, Marseilles." The *SS* stood for Section Sanitaire (medical service unit), the *U* for Etats-Unis. Our outgoing letters and postcards bore this return address and the stencil *FM* (Franchise Militaire) in lieu of stamps. They were also censored and bore the further imprint "Contrôle Postal Militaire." Sometimes we could speed our letters home by having them mailed in Paris by a fellow driver returning there at the end of his engagement with us. In those days civilian mail home required a 25-centime stamp for a letter and 10 centimes for a postcard.

Parcels eagerly awaited included periodicals, books, knitted items, and delicacies. In one of my letters home from Bistrika I observed: "Like Thackeray's school boys writing home for plumcake, I must say that I would like to get some *sugar* when that cold from the hills strikes this place about November first. Besides, tea without sugar is medicine." A now-forgotten heroine of World War I was the *marraine de guerre*. A number of our drivers were adopted beneficiaries of American women living in Europe, active in hospital or canteen service, who, like my Miss Stanley, sent us packages and supposedly sustained our morale.

Reading matter received from home made its rounds among our various tents and burrows. In one entry in my journal I note receipt of issues of *Judge* and *The New Republic* and a section of the *New York Times*. Books could be sent, though when I was in the army later they could only get through if the covers were torn off and they were rolled up like magazines. A number of the drivers were assiduous students. One loaned me a thousand-page textbook on physiology which I kept at for weeks. The French lieutenant, who had received two degrees in Paris, had a collection of French classics, and met with me regularly as I worked on French composition. The Virginia blueblood Brodaux Cameron (Princeton) had a small library. I finished *Vanity Fair*, a life of John Bright, and works of William James and Bertrand Russell. In French I had been reading Molière, Bossuet, *Les Misérables*, Flaubert's *Tentation de St. Antoine*, and Renan.

Some of us had started to learn modern Greek on the way out but never got very far with it. Our French, however, which we used a good deal in our duties, served us later when we returned to France to join various U.S. Army units. When my artillery regiment, after training, first entered the lines at Les Eparges, south of Verdun, in March 1918, I was called up out of the ranks to ride as an interpreter with the colonel and a French liaison officer as they positioned our batteries.

Like all French units the Section received such rations as the army: canned beef called "monkey meat" (*singe!*), dried vegetables (especially lentils), bread, coffee, and wine (*pinard*). The Field Service supplemented this diet by purchases in civilian markets like Florina. Because the American drivers had an anomalous status between common soldier and officer, our field kitchen orderly could draw upon what special supplies might be available for the latter. Thus fresh beef, vegetables, fruit, and condensed milk sometimes surprised us. The cook could do wonders with what was available. When I was with Section 2 earlier we had a chef who had formerly been chief cook at the Café de la Paix in Paris, and we hailed his accomplishments.

The social life and camaraderie of our encampment in that ravine— like a lumber camp in the wilds—reflected the high spirits of the volunteers and the diversity of their talents and backgrounds. Most were college undergraduates who wanted to be where the action was, impelled by a love of adventure, but also by an unarticulated commitment. Displaced thousands of miles, they had transferred from campus and playing fields to this different theatre their youthful ebullience and enterprise. Here also, of course, their zest and companionship in the enterprise were heightened by the element of danger. If this was like a lumber camp or a mining operation in Wyoming, this camp was in the shadow of a volcano.

The makeup and quality of the section, as of the Field Service generally, was no doubt distinctive, if not superior, by comparison with college students generally. In those days undergraduates did not break up their four-year course or take a junior year abroad. It was only by a special exception that deans and faculties granted us leaves of absence for ambulance service. In our case their reluctance was overcome because local groups of prominent citizens sponsored the program. In Boston and New York and at the Ivy League schools these circles overlapped with those who sympathized with the Allies and opposed Woodrow Wilson's efforts to keep the United States out of war. In California, for example, where there was a strong "America-first" isolationist sentiment, a vigorous group at the University of California at Berkeley and at Stanford University backed the Field Service, donated cars, and mobilized volunteers. Charles Mills Gayley, the distinguished English literature scholar at Berkeley, was one of the prime movers of this initiative.[6]

Isolationism in the United States in this period before America entered the war took curious forms. When I was in Section 2 in March 1917 a statement in a Philadelphia paper claimed that Americans serving in the Allied armies were no longer American citizens in point of law. This item, received through the mail by one of our number, led to a fevered consultation among the drivers and an initiative which became notorious in the annals of the section. We had a flamboyant fellow driver named Ewen MacIntyre, Jr., from Brighton, Mass., not a college man, but something of a journalist and versifier, who was widely known in the Service for his "Song of the Soixante-Quinze."[7] MacIntyre wrote a letter which we were all to sign which began as follows:

March 28, 1917

At the Front

The Honorable Theodore Roosevelt:

To you, the Representative American, we address our wrongs. In the columns of the Philadelphia Public Ledger, for February 14th, appeared these words: "Americans who have joined the armies of the Allies as aviators or ambulance drivers are no longer American citizens in point of law."

We are members of Section 2 of the American Ambulance, "a petal of that finest flower of the magnificent wreath offered by the great America to her little Latin sister." [This was taken from a public tribute to the Field Service by one of Joffre's staff.]

Is this disquieting notice. . . .

In my journal I noted that MacIntyre and his co-editors intended to send this letter to the Paris *Herald* and to Roosevelt, but I have no further record of it.

In any case, those who dropped their studies to join the Service were somewhat exceptional. Their forwardness in action was combined with a fund of America's fabled resourcefulness and buoyancy. The diversity of types and backgrounds made for an exhilarating association at meals and in the shelters. Patrician families were represented in many of the sections. In Section 2 we had an Ames of Boston and two Chew brothers of Philadelphia, and Section 10, in Albania, had its New York Rhinelander. In our own section we had a representative of the Verrills, a leading family of Portland, Maine, and a Cameron of Petersburg, Virginia, who regaled us with accounts of his post-Civil War forebears in the watering places of the Old Dominion. Noblesse oblige could be recognized as a patriotic motivation in this whole adventure beyond the seas. But equally evident, as in the case of the Lafayette Escadrille, were the cases of extraordinary native capacity and leadership which emerged in the corps, a testimony to the democratic potential of our society. Later in a U.S. Field Artillery battery I observed this same dynamism and versatility in the ranks. It was often the personal force and contagious drive of our noncommissioned officers that sustained the morale of the crews and carried them over obstacles, even in units commanded by West Point officers.

In committing themselves to this faraway cauldron of war these young American volunteers could not well visualize what was ahead. Though their engagement was for noncombatant duty, and for a limited term, the theatre was strange and eventualities were hidden. Despite the excellence of the organization of the Service, this was not like signing up for a field trip or mining camp in the tropics. Not only had there been casualties since 1915 but the course of the war itself was unpredictable. In sober fact we young cubs and tyros did not know what we were getting into. In this respect we only anticipated the hosts of Americans who began to arrive in France in the fall of 1917 for whom both the scene and the future were unknown. No doubt the zest of our activities was linked with this sense of venture. Some of us were solely animated by a quest for excitement, and a few here and there in the sections could be recognized by their mixed backgrounds and rootlessness as professional soldiers of fortune. One of our favorite songs was Kipling's "Gentlemen-Rankers":

> We're poor little lambs who've lost our way,
> Baa! Baa! Baa!
> We're little black sheep who've gone astray,
> Baa–aa–aa!
> Gentlemen-rankers out on a spree
> Damned from here to Eternity,
> God ha' mercy on such as we,
> Baa! Yah! Bah!

In any case those of us who had abandoned our studies at home soon found that our remote involvement opened up many unforeseen outcomes. Those of us in Section 3 could well rub our eyes and ask how we had come to be in the mountains of Macedonia. Still more unexpected was that sequence of events which led to the involvement of most of us with the American field artillery and aviation in 1918.

Meanwhile, as individuals we encountered our own hazards and surprises. A fellow driver in Section 2 was stricken with spinal meningitis his first night at the front. Two of our companions in Section 3—Waller Harrison of Oberlin and William Emerson of Harvard—lost their lives after enlisting in the Army, as did our Lieutenant Derode after rejoining the French army. Well known is the anomalous case of the poet E. E. Cummings, who had an unfortunate contre-temps with the French authorities when a volunteer ambulance driver (not with the AFS) and had to return home after detention in "the enormous room," the title of his recollection of the war.

The most unexpected turn of events for hundreds of ambulance volunteers in 1917 was to be diverted to camion service. There was such a shortage in the French automobile service of lorry drivers that our headquarters in Paris prevailed on the arriving recruits to sacrifice the romance of their enlistment and drive trucks rather than ambulances. The names of these crestfallen comrades are properly listed in the roster of the Field Service with the rest of us. Thus along with "SSU 3" there appear such designations as "Malcolm Cowley TMU 526" (short for Transport Matériel U.S., Section 526). This branch of our service to the French armies had its own arduous and dangerous ordeals, as its fourteen sections delivered countless munition and supplies to the lines, necessary especially in the critical attacks and jeopardies of the summer of 1917.[8]

My journal evokes many features of the camaraderie and gusto of life in the encampment near Monastir. Every such group has its characters —in ours notably Gilbert Sinclair of Montana, an imperturbable mountain of a man known as "the Sphinx." His taciturnity, laconic ironies, and eruptive rough-housing only further incited the delighted persiflage at his expense. The only time the Sphinx was ever at a loss was when he returned flabbergasted from his driving test on the hairpin turns over the precipices above Slivika. The western states were represented in our company by Amsden of New Mexico and Varnum of Idaho, both Harvard students who had the colorful traits of ranch and rodeo. Like Sinclair they later served in the U.S. aviation corps.

The conversation at meals under the larger tent revolved about incidents of the service and, as the fall approached, rumors about the takeover of our work by the French and our return to Paris. One driver would tell of a broken axle at night far from any telephone. Another described driving in the eye of an enemy searchlight. (In my journal I recorded carrying a *"projecteur-malade,"* that is, one of our own French searchlight operators, who told me that the danger of being spotted is small until after the "playing" of his beam.) Card games went on in our dugout shelters. Those who had delicacies from home or from the markets in Florina convoked others for cocoa or tea. (Missing here were the cognac or champagne sometimes available for our parties in Section 2 in the Argonne.) Berkeley Michael, a Princeton driver, had somehow acquired a phonograph. Photos were developed and printed in our burrows. As September approached, we had signs of the rainy season and winter to come, and we spent a great deal of time reinforcing our shelters.

August 31. [Letter home] Yesterday two of the boys started at 3 A.M. for a walk to the snow and ridge behind us, very high and remote. From the top they could see the lines for miles, as well as Lake Presba and the back country toward Salonika. They won their bets too by getting back well within 20 hours. The only person they saw way up there was a Serb gathering snow for one of the hospitals down here—their fever patients. I wouldn't have believed there would be snow anywhere in this heat in August.

Today we got an order to "Fill up, everybody—tank and reserve." A good sized attack had been prophesied for the near future. These expectations are usually vain. If there is one, the guns will be busier with the batteries and lines than with the roads—which just suits us.

Bistrika, Sept. 2. [Journal] For three hours a Bulgar bombardment of French battery 4 or 5 hundred yards from hospital, threw *éclats* into the yard. Took a boy to the English Hospital where a nurse showed me wards of civilian *blessés* there cared for. In the hall was a woman 90 years old and a child of six weeks (mother killed—baby with a broken arm) both Serbian . . . [I took] 5 *assis* to Florina.

Sept. 4. [Letter home] Here's a little variety. Since August 31 there has been an Allied *coup de main* every night on one or another of the lines about Monastir. The turn of our division came last night. Of course the medical service was given advanced information. So last night at 7, altho' everything about is as quiet as Sunday at home, in roll 8 or 10 ambulances to the Hospital Court, an unheard of number. When it gets real dark they steal out to a couple of new advanced *postes*. Cameron and I had been sent up at 2 P.M. to be on duty at the hospital. We were left stranded there, with our "mech," Roberts, almost as envious and disappointed as Sinclair and the others who were *en repos* at camp. But as it turned out, we got the fun not the others . . .

Roberts and I were talking in front of my car about 9:30, the only ones in the court, when one of a number of shells that had been seeking out a near French battery came so far astray as to fall in the yard 100 feet from us. I was curled up on my running board, and Roberts stretched out on the ground by that time. I never heard such a vicious shriek or such a noise. My soul scattered into as many atoms as the shell. I looked up and saw a great whirling black wall of dust not twenty feet off, towering like a genie.

My journal entry for September 3 supplements this account.

Suddenly a whistle altogether different, vicious crescendo, closer, closer, terrible stupefying. I telescope myself on the running board, Roberts on the ground. Surely it's all over for us. Then a roar, world-crashing that seems to come out from inside one, so enveloping it is, and one's soul dissipated into atoms . . . Robt. gets up saying kind of dazily, "That was pretty close—are you all right." I laughed quite light-heartedly—one doesn't realize these things—and wondered out loud if the car had been touched.

After this close shave in the hospital yard and before the cars began
to come in with casualties from the French raid, I was sent to pick up a
couple of doctors at Velusina (18 kilometers distant). My journal entry
for September 3 continues:

Getting back at 1 A.M. I saw the cars coming in steadily with freshly
wounded men, sitting and lying. Perhaps 40 *couchés* and 20 *assis*.
Cost of a *coup-de-main*. About 2 A.M. they began to be evacuated to
Florina. At 3:30 I left with 1 *couché* and 3 *assis*—the last car—and
went very slowly. The dawn came on after an hour's driving. When
we were rid of our loads and had gotten our stretchers back we were
as tickled as a lot of boys on holiday, and raced up to camp to get
some condensed milk [for our coffee] before it was all gone.

Sept. 14. This morning the whole valley and mts. are covered or
screened with great masses of mist and cloud of all shades from
pure white to thunder black, with a little blue sky. The hills—blue-
black above, or red where weathered, or straw where furze—with
the reflections, are a study in magnificence. Last night an electric storm, besides flashes from a distant artillery duel between low
clouds and stars, over the mountains.

Lots of Greeks going up to the lines these days. My *projecteur*
friend says that they were the best kind of soldiers, noting especially their invincible habit of singing. . . . He says that they do it
in the front lines.

My little mouse, who wakes me up so often at night breaking into
my larder, fell into my water-pitcher last night and nearly drowned.
Perhaps he was badly enough scared to confine himself to Tom
Lowry's shack [next door] after this.

As the season wore on rumors multiplied that we were to be replaced.
My journal reflects our uncertainty. On September 25 a number of us
"gather tiles from Monastir ruins for dry-footing here in the rainy season." On the twenty-seventh we hear that the Ambulance Service in
France had been taken over by the U.S. Army. On October first I stroll
with Jimmie Todd in Monastir, looking for curios and souvenirs: Turkish
coffee pots, wooden spoons, and sandals. Work is lighter. There is men-

tion of bridge games, photography, parties with chocolate and gateaux, and packages from home.

Oct. 9. To Monastir, on duty with Tom Lowry. Very dark. To the *poste* at Grand Rocher. Big shell holes, 4 or 5 feet deep along the road, as big as a car. 5 trips: 3 to Greek hospital . . . Out till 3 a.m. Crescent moon, broken sky, searchlight, starshells, minarets, white plaster, locusts.

Oct. 13. 19 French drivers here to replace us . . . Lumen [Tenney] took out one on his trip. He hit 3 teams on his way home. —My car inventoried and given over to a French driver for good. —The last drive taken, alas.

Oct. 14. Went off up the ridge for a day with Renan and a pocket lunch. Got up on a high outlook where I could see aeroplane thrills, bombardment about Monastir, and the length and breadth of the valley. Two Serb boys with French military articles in their garb and long smooth staffs strolled up while their large flocks of cows and sheep made angel music beyond the brow of the hill. Every sheep a bell, every bell a different tone. Altogether in that distant silent place, possessing an enchantment.

We evacuated our camp site and shelters at Bistrika on October 17, entraining at Florina for Salonika.

Oct. 18. [Letter to Thornton] We are lolling on our baggage in the station in Salonika, just arrived from Monastir after a 24 hrs trip on the ravitaillement [military supply] train. Jack D'Este, our *chef* is up town making arrangements for our further travel and immediate quarters. "Harry" (Waller Harrison) is reading a miniature copy of Julius Caesar. Lumen [Tenney] is sound asleep with a newspaper over his face on a pile of trunks and blanket rolls. Jimmie is next to me stirring occasionally to dislodge the flies. Five of the boys are at a game of bridge at so much the point in the waiting room. There is no covered platform, but a row of locust trees between the brick station and "Track 1." Farther up is a French Captain—3 stripes. Then there are Greek, Italian, French and Russians—officers and

men. The most unusual are the Anam soldiers from Indo-China.
When a Russian goes by he is followed by vituperation [Russia had
now pulled out of the war]. The Greeks are most in evidence, tho'
the French control things in this Greek city. A Greek complained
that while French horses rode on the railway (Greek), Greek officers
walked. . . .
French soldiers boarding a train to return to France on *permission*
[leave] are shouting and singing. They are almost tearfully happy.
A bunch of Zouaves in red fezes board a train for Monastir and the
front. The cars on the tracks before me are of all nations (like the
coins we use)—Greek, French, English and German. Most of them
say "40 men or six horses." They are loaded with great sacks, or
casks of wine, broken-down autos, new-painted two-wheeled carts,
fuel, hay, soldiers. The station itself is quiet enough. Beside it is
an *abri* in case of bombardment. There is a tent to receive the
blessés from the *"trains sanitaires"* coming in from Florina and
Exisu. Behind the station the strange city begins with its cafes,
Serbian milk kitchens, fish-frying stalls, fruit stands, venders,
etc. The street car runs runs here to the East end of town, passing
under the *Arc de Triumph de Galerius* and turning at right angles
toward the sea which it meets at the White Tower on the Quai . . .
Inside the city are the *"sinistres"* or ruins of the fire [the great conflagration of August 18].

Oct. 19. [Letter continuing] We stayed at the "Parc Autos Reserve"
last night. Today I walked the town. The very heart of the city is
burned out—the centers of the former "Parisian Life"—the big
Hotel ("Splendide"), the big cafe, the two movie shows, the big
business offices. So too block after block of Macedonian shops and
dwellings, the hives of the little people. The ruins of fire here ex-
ceed infinitely the ruins by shell and bomb in Monastir, even as this
great city excels that community. Fire, earthquake, pestilence and
famine are the co-workers of War. The most famous building in the
city, Church of St. Demitrius, is a broken shell . . . The building
has only come again into the hands of the Greek Christian Church
since the Turks were expelled in 1912. The outer Moslem plasters

have been removed and the ancient Christian mural paintings disclosed. The fire of this summer has with its destruction brought the discovery of a crypt below the chapel—wherein are interesting things. Pictures of Demetrius. Scares of the game of knuckle-bone, scratched by the masons in their hours off work.

We left Salonika on October 19 in two boxcars, and passing Larissa we journeyed to Bralo (near Lamia). On the twenty-first (exactly one year after my departure from New York to join the Paris Service in 1916) we joined a long convoy, traveling in two camions for four hours over the recently constructed military road to Itia on the Gulf of Corinth. This road through the mountains had been built to obviate the long and dangerous transport by sea around the Peloponnesus.

I spent the night of October 21 in Itia in shelter described in my journal as "an overcrowded stable, open on one side, with a dirt floor and upper gallery." With us were a great "push of *poilus*" on their way north to the Macedonian front. A letter home of Oct. 23 recalls a sleepless night.

It was most disillusioning. It was obscene. I couldn't look a French soldier in the face the next day. War makes brutes of these men. Besides drunkeness, profanity, hilarity, etc. there was a fight between two men that seemed on the point of taking a serious turn— and none interferred [officers or military police] . . . all night long something was going on.

In retrospect I note that this disabusing scene opened up a subsoil, indeed, an ordinarily veiled gulf in men at war: bitterness, loathing, anguish, paroxysm. After three years in the trenches, still caught in the swamp of war, they were now on their way to a new zone of fire. Here, as in a prison riot, circumstances afforded license for the irruption of despair, cynicism, and malignity. But it would be a mistake to think that these lavas are confined to men at war. Moreover, it was these same men in horizon blue or their likes who had sustained the ordeals of the Marne, Verdun, and the Chemin des Dames.

These contradictions were part of our experience in the Field Service. Most of us in the AFS were undoubtedly naive as we entered this great convulsion of Europe and the nations. The ingenuousness of youth was subject to a kind of forced maturing in our tasks, but inevitably the idealism we had brought to the engagement was sobered by our initiation. Both the disabusing traits of human nature and the atrocious ravages of war combined to unsettle our naiveté.

This reassessment, however, did not mean a total disenchantment with the war or with the cause of France and the Allies. Our reactions at the time did, indeed, anticipate what became general in the sequel of World War I, a recognition of how superficially and fraudulently the rhetoric of patriotism and heroism and sacrifice had been invoked. We were early disabused of propaganda and its simplistic clichés; we were alert to the sophistries of flag-waving and crusades. But this did not lead us to a blanket condemnation of the war as it did later for so many of our countrymen, motivated in some circles by a disappointed idealism, in others by cynicism or ideology. Most of the Field Service volunteers, after their sections were militarized, enlisted as I did in combatant units of the American Expeditionary Forces.

The following day, October 22, we were ferried with a large contingent of French troops to an old tramp steamer, *The Mustapha*, where we were crowded with our baggage into a dining saloon. Throughout this return trip to France we travelled as privates, though on our journey in July a resourceful French lieutenant had been able to pass us off as aviators (in view of our officer-like uniforms) so that we had certain privileges. Returning, we shared the crowded lot of the ranks on the boat and in the barracks in Tarentum while our *chef* (group leader) and *sous-chef* had a stateroom on board and went to a hotel when we debarked. There was much grumbling about our *chef* as earlier in camp, and I have always thought that when a few Croix de guerres were subsequently doled out to our section, I received one mainly because I did not speak up like some of the others.

In my journal I noted that this day of our sailing was "the second day of headache." This was the harbinger of the bad case of malaria. In the crowded situation of our quarters, all of us wearing life-belts, it was difficult to rest. We were in Tarentum from October 23 to 28, as I continued to be nauseated. Like Brodaux Cameron I went to a local military hospital. His malaria kept him there over two weeks, but I was able to go on with the group on a troop train, lying on the floor of the *wagon sanitaire*, a converted mail car. Henry Rubinkam (University of Chicago), Bob Verrill, and Gil Sinclair brought in a gasoline heater and compounded applesauce for me. Finally, after arrival at Livorno and a night at a hotel there, Jack D'Este agreed I should not try to go on with the rest, and I was moved to a *sous-officiers* ward of the French military hospital, which had a continuing contingent of casualties from the crowded troop trains coming and going daily.

This interruption of my journey back to Paris could not have occurred at a better place. During the seven days of my treatment there, first on the *petit régime* as my appetite returned, I got in touch with my aunt Charlotte Niven (my mother's sister) in Florence. She had for some years been busy in YWCA work first in Naples and then in Florence, and was now overextended with assistance to the refugees crowding into the city in consequence of the collapse of the Italian front at Caporetto. The *medicin-chef* at Livorno granted me a convalescent leave of four days to Florence.

The vicissitudes of war service could have these compensating surprises and interludes. A dusty and exhausted convoy like one I recall could catch a glimpse in the distance of the towers of the cathedral of Beauvais or of Reims, or find itself in the neighborhood of Domrémy. I had just recently passed close to Delphi in our convoy to Itia but in this case without knowing it. But here I was in Florence. The preceding May on my short leave from Section 2 in Paris I had been able to wangle a week in the English Lake District with blanket and canteen by wrestling with both French and British bureaus for the necessary passes. Thus I exchanged the ravines of the Argonne for the shores of Grasmere and Rydal Water.

This time I had exited as through a looking-glass from the network of military control, which stretched across Europe, into the worlds of Giotto, Dante, and Michelangelo—but also of Ruskin and Browning. My aunt had her apartment in the home of the Blakes, James Blake being the padre of the Scottish church in Florence and an authority on the arts and history of the city. Among other things he was an early mover in the project to secure Casa Guidi, the former home of Robert and Elizabeth Browning, and to endow it as a shrine for pilgrims to the Browning sites in Italy. I had taken William Lyon Phelps' famous course on Tennyson and Browning at Yale, and could inform him (through my family) of my pilgrimage to Florence in wartime. Billy Phelps had long kept a record of those former members of his course who advised him by postcard of their visits to Asola and Florence.

In my journal I briefly recorded our visits to many famous shrines and collections. The Uffizzi was closed. In the Pitti Palace the glass had been removed from the paintings in case of bombardment. The Duomo, San Marco, San Lorenzo, and other landmarks were all as I was to know them later. Fiesole with its Etruscan wall and Roman theater evoked earlier epochs, while in the present the talk was all of the recent disaster at Caporetto. The attack there had begun on October 24th. After the most critical days, October 30 and 31, the situation was slowly stabilized by rushed Allied reinforcements and supplies. Meanwhile, refugees scattered widely, and my aunt was busy with one of the many *foyers* which cared for them. Now, as I write after seventy years, those days in Florence remain all but irretrievable for me, again like the oldest obliterated legend of a palimpsest.

After this parenthesis I resumed my journey to Paris.

Monday, Nov. 12. Livorno to Genoa in a freight-car with 17 others—*sous-officiers* and *poilus*. Slept on a bench.

Tuesday, 13th. Omiglia to Marseilles. At Cannes, train after train of English troops from Ypres go by—thousands of men, with artillery, etc., on their way to the Italian front. Our French *poilus* shout to them, "N'allez-pas là-bas!" imitating cattle. [In other words: "Don't go down there; they'll make mince-meat of you."]

Marseilles [From a letter home.] We reached a station outside Marseilles at midnight. From there we marched three miles through the silent streets—a thousand of us—to the barracks for troops passing through the city. It was cold sleeping, but I felt my heart strangely warmed at being lost in such a great crowd of *poilus*. They were all very good to me, recognizing me as an American *engagé voluntaire*.

Wednesday, 14th. Bath in Marseilles. Train at 12:45 P.M. Arrived Paris. To rue Raynouard [Field Service headquarters].

Paris, Nov. 26. Enlisted [as private] in the U.S. Field Artillery for the "emergency" at 10 Rue St. Anne and passed my physical exam.

Buick-Six ambulances parked in courtyard of the American Ambulance Hospital, the former Lycée Pasteur, at Neuilly-sur-Seine, near Paris, November 1916. Amos N. Wilder's duties as driver involved moving casualties from trains to hospitals throughout the city. All photographs taken by Amos N. Wilder or with his Brownie camera.

Wilder's fellow American Field Service (AFS) drivers at a poste de secours in the trenches of the Argonne, March 1917. From these locations casualties were evacuated to hospital facilities in and near Paris.

AFS drivers at La Grange aux Bois, the headquarters of Section 2, in the Argonne, April 1917. Wilder is third from left.

Loading horses in French boxcars, spring 1917. Wilder would directly encounter this recurring ordeal after joining the American Expeditionary Forces.

Wilder (lower left) and fellow drivers of Section 3 in the train at Tarentum on their way to Macedonia for service with the Army of the Orient, July 1917.

*August 1917 view of Bistrika, Section 3 AFS encampment in valley outside Mona-
stir with "rolling kitchen" on right, tented eating area, and storage and auto repair structures to left. Drivers built and lived in dugouts on the far hillside above
road they called "Fifth Avenue."*

*Wilder on the Monastir-Florina evacuation route. This Ser-
bian nurse, frightened of Americans, insisted on a Serbian
army escort who was forced, by lack of space, to perch on the
running board for the twenty-mile trip.*

Wilder on the eyries of the Balkans above Monastir, September 1917.

Model-T ambulances in the courtyard of the Monastir field hospital where Wilder was nearly killed by a shell in the summer of 1917.

Corporal Wilder after the Armistice in a photo taken at the fortress of Ehrenbreitstein in 1919.

* * *

Part Two

With the American
Expeditionary Forces in
the Field Artillery

After the takeover of the ambulance sections by the U.S. Army, the erstwhile volunteer drivers were free to continue with their sections, now "federalized" in our Expeditionary Force and no longer under French authority, or to seek enlistment in some other branch of the service. Our two Field Service sections in the Balkans, however, could not continue under our flag as the United States was then not at war with Austria and Bulgaria. By the time of my return to the legendary headquarters of the Field Service at 21 rue Raynouard in Passy, operations there had been closing down.

I look on my enlistment in the more active military involvement of our army as the logical sequel of my volunteering with the ambulance service a year earlier in November 1916. American participation in the European struggle, an intervention now taking on a momentous significance, had had its antecedents and forerunners in the several volunteer corps which had pioneered this reinforcement of the French and British armies and their cause, among these initiatives the American Field Service. To venture an analogy, the American Field Service was like the pilot-fish showing the way to the American Leviathan.[1]

By the time I returned to Paris the second week of November 1917 a number of Americans in military uniforms of all ranks were to be seen in the city. On the train from Marseilles I had talked with young lieutenants, graduates of Princeton and Williams, who had received training and commissions at our Plattsburgh ROTC and who had just completed further training at a camp near Lyons. Several others were on their way back from short leaves on the Riviera. Such compatriots, either on duty or in transit in Paris, thronged such hospitality centers as the YMCA hotels in the boulevards where meals and entertainments were provided. They sat at ease at the tables in the cafés and sauntered in the Tuileries and the Champs Elysées with a characteristic nonchalance and self-possession as of a breed which could take care of any difficulty or annoyance like that of the impasse of the war. When they got to the front they named their howitzers "Peace Talk" and "Hang the Kaiser." The extenuated French after three years of war could not but hail this sublime self-assurance and innocence in their new cohorts.

After my release from the ambulance service I was busy for some days pending my enlistment with farewells, last walks in the Bois de Boulogne, Christmas gifts for the family at home, deposit of my belongings, including transfer of my civilian clothing, at the American Express office. At this time the family was living in Mt. Carmel, eight miles from New Haven. My brother, Thornton, was in his junior year at Yale, my sister Charlotte was a sophomore at Mount Holyoke, and my younger sisters, Isabel and Janet, were at home.

The letterhead on which this letter home was written bears the triangular shield of the American YMCA, with the legend, "On Active Service with the A.E.F."

Paris, Nov. 15, 1917

At Rue Raynouard I got my release . . . They are very courteous to their old boys here especially if they have been with the Field Service as long as I have. So I can make my home here for a week in their barracks and have my meals there, pending my new engagement. The place is much changed. When I left here for Salonika in July the Field Service was growing by leaps and bounds, and crowded with new-comers and old drivers. Now [the Sections having been federalized] it is static, merely maintained in its present condition, with the boys all scattered and signing up for their new enlistments.

This afternoon I had a bike ride for a couple of hours—part of my plan for getting in condition for my physical examination. Tonight there is a supper and entertainment here at the Y.M.C.A. Hotel in the Boulevard district. I am waiting for Jimmie Todd [Oberlin, Section 3] before going in to "manger." Over my head is a sign: "When did you write your mother last?" The quite luxurious hotel is running over with Americans in uniform of all branches—all evidently straight from hot baths and strolling about in typical American self-possession. It's great to see them.

During these days I explored the possibility of getting a commission in the Field Artillery together with assignment to an officers' training school. With the assistance of Professor George H. Nettleton of Yale, then director of the American University Union in Europe in Paris, I secured letters of recommendation to the adjutant general at Pershing's headquarters in Chaumont from influential army officers. At this time I received a delayed notification of some ambiguous citation accorded me by the French division which I had served in Serbia, which turned out to be a Croix de guerre.* Though I was puzzled by this distinction and eulogy—a roll of the dice in the lottery with which our French division chose to honor several drivers of our departing Section 3, many of whom were more worthy than myself—I was glad to include this with my credentials for a commission. My petition at Chaumont proved fruitless.

*Amos Wilder's Croix de guerre citation, bestowed on October 28, 1917, reads as follows in translation: "An American ambulance driver in the service of France since January 1917, twice a volunteer,—on the French front, and in the Army of the Orient; he has on all occasions, and especially at the Monastir sector, shown absolute devotion and perfect intrepidity in the service of our wounded."

"Lack of military service" debarred me from such advancement. After I had proved myself in active service in the ranks I could apply again.

I was not greatly disappointed. As my letters home indicated, my convictions about the war prized an immediate and full identification with our national mission in the ranks. I felt it specially urgent that Americans of privileged families and schooling should do their part with the conscripted hosts of all classes, breeds, and occupations who were drawn into the conflict. Though I found that I was almost the only college-trained youth in the battery to which I was thereafter assigned, apart from our officers, I soon recognized the superlative talents, fiber, and commitment of many of our common doughboys and noncommissioned officers.

Contacts in Paris during these days with other Field Service veterans revealed the variety of options open at the time. One continued in his section because he failed in the physical examination to qualify for a more active branch of the service. Philip Rhinelander, a former Thacher School friend who had served in Section 10 in Albania, entered our aviation corps and later lost his life at the front. Friends from Oberlin went to England and joined the Royal Flying Corps.

On November 26 I enlisted as a private in the U.S. Artillery "for the emergency" at our recruiting office, 11 rue Ste.-Anne, near the Opéra Comique. This step, like that in any army, and in distinction from my Field Service engagement, like the oath of a monk or nun entering a religious order, impressed me as involving a radical abrogation of personal freedom and autonomy. In the exigencies of war the soldier in all eras surrenders individual liberty of action to the chain of command. Yet his latent motivations, as indeed in the case of slaves and convicts, still have their theatre, all the more so when, as in this case, they are linked with the original decision.

My enlistment was accompanied by a rigorous physical examination, one which reassured me that my recent spell of malaria was now well over. Inevitably one of the tests was for venereal disease. This unpleasant inquisition was recurrent in the army at those times when we were in the rear and the men were free for promiscuity in the village cafés or visits to the French-licensed and supposedly controlled brothels. This reminds me that in Paris I encountered solicitous American women who distributed little medallions of Sir Galahad and Joan of Arc to passing soldiers, thus prompting our abstinence from other kinds of solicitation.

At this time my sister Charlotte at Mount Holyoke was exploring ways of getting into some kind of service in France. I wrote to my mother Nov. 23:

> Let Charlotte come by all means. Miss Stanley says the finest work in the war that girls can do is merely to live in Paris and give themselves to meeting and serving the American soldiers over here that crave feminine companionship and go to the worst places for it if it is to be found nowhere else. One Canadian said to me, "I came in here and a lady spoke to me. I was so overcome that it was some minutes, I assure you, before I could answer her." He had been away from the gracious side of life for many months in the trenches.

At the time of my medical checkup on Nov. 26 I ran into another volunteer, Fred Gale (from Harvard), who had served with a camion (lorry) section. In a letter home, I narrated his story:

> Gale never fired a gun in his life, of a blushing and rosy countenance, was with me in taking our physical examination. He wanted to go into the infantry (private) for no special reason except that he wanted to be "in it," bait, hook and sinker. He did poorly in the eye test. The doctor didn't know whether to let him by. It was life or death for Gale because he was going home if he couldn't pass. The doctor asked him with a touch of irony, "You want in bad, do you?" Gale replied, "If you pass me, I'll go in; if not I'll go home." The doctor said to come back next morning. I wonder if Gale slept. When I turned up next morning at the Salle d'Attendance, Gale was just going to learn his fate. He came out with a bit of excitement on his face and said, "He won't pass me!"

I was later surprised to find Gale assigned to the artillery and on my train to a training camp. The doctor had evidently consented to his service in this branch, judging that he was not the type for the infantry. Gale was in fact a highly qualified musician, having studied with Arthur

Foote at home. While in Paris he had looked up the leading organists and organs in the churches of the city. In our training camp he was a great asset at the piano in the entertainments and theatricals put on by our YMCA program. After the war I saw something of Fred Gale in his native Gloucester, Massachusetts, when I went to visit Blanche Stanley at her summer studio in East Gloucester.

My next formality was that of reporting to the quartermaster's depot (November 28) where I presumed I would be outfitted with uniform and other equipment. All that they could give me for the moment was three blankets. But when it came to my next destination the recruiting officer was at a loss. As I was a "casual" signed up for the artillery but not assigned to any particular unit, they did not know what to do with me. In short, I was "a new case." A letter home reports details of this period when I was in limbo.

> Sitting in the Q.M.'s office I caught a glimpse of the wide range and enormity of the task of this department. Here's a telephone call for eating utensils. Here is a complaint that in France one can't get *pie crust* for Thanksgiving American army pumpkin pie (a serious matter). Here's a claim for travel expenses with orders all balled up.

Our Virginia blueblood in Section 3 in Macedonia, Brodaux Cameron, turned up at the recruiting office when I was there. I recounted the episode in a letter home.

> Cameron brought a storm of abuse down on himself by his assured attitude in the recruiting room. He expostulated over the delays, etc., and then found that he was "in the wrong pew," since he was looking for a commission. [Cameron must have received his commission since the record shows that he ended up as an instructor in a U.S. Aviation School.] College men are generally mistrusted by the regulars [i.e., old soldiers long in the army]. "I don't believe in your damned draft, either," said the orderly to a couple of us. "A man that has to be drafted ain't good enough for this army." He had big feet, big hands and a coarse face somewhat relieved by a good-humored turned-up nose.

On this same occasion I myself got typhoid and para-typhoid shots in my left arm and smallpox vaccination in my right, and then had to sleep on a barracks floor that way, for an orderly had brought me by métro way out to an eastern suburb of Paris to my first army quarters. This was an ancient park of regimental barracks, at Remilly, which must have gone back to the time of Napoleon. With me was an old American engineer just out of a hospital after being gassed and exposed to snow and rain while in railroad construction near the front. The few other occupants were mainly French. I was given a place and eventually a bunk in an immense bare room on the fifth floor. While I stayed here still in limbo for some days I availed myself of the laxity of regulations and went back into the city where I saw friends, went to the opera, and finally received my uniform and other equipment. During these weeks I was reading *The Cloister and the Hearth*, De Quincey, *M. Beaucaire*, and Descartes. In the months to come such fare would be largely restricted.

Valdahon and the Seventeenth Field Artillery

Provisional assignment and travel orders were finally received. I was to report to the American commandant at the Artillery Training Center at Valdahon which was near Besançon and the Swiss border.[2] I departed December 3 from the Gare de l'Est and reached this destination, after two changes, late in the day. The post with its barracks and extensive firing range was at the time inactive pending the arrival of the artillery brigade in which I was to serve. Meanwhile, it was manned by an interim personnel of the Sixth Artillery Regiment to whose headquarters company I was assigned. My billet was in a squad room with a dozen orderlies, staff car drivers, and dispatch riders. But there were also two former ambulance men, Henry Wharton of Section 16 and Gordon Bartlett from another volunteer corps. I found myself immediately submerged in the peremptory disciplines and protocols of army life: reveille while it was still dark, chow line, policing quarters, salutes and inspections, squad duties at kitchen or stables, service with various "details," drill, and so on until "retreat" at the end of the day.

Our sergeant-major by exception was not of the martinet kind who enforce their orders by oaths, profanity, and sarcasm. He was of a quiet type whose authority was enforced by a nod. In the squad room or on the parade ground he would issue an order, looking at the ground, accompanied by a jerk of the head. There was less entertainment for the ranks in this kind of discipline, but it was more effective.

Gordon Bartlett was a Dartmouth student whose father and family were associated with the work in Japan of one of our most distinguished Congregational Boards of Foreign Missions, notable for its long educational and medical service in the Far East. In our squad room Gordon kneeled down to say his prayers before lights out. A tough dispatch-rider in another bed hereupon jeered and threw a boot at him. When he had finished his prayers Bartlett stood up and confronted his ribald persecutor, ready to do battle then and there. Though the culprit was a hardened veteran of long service in the army, he turned to blustering and then backed down. Bartlett could have licked any two of them. He later lost his life in action in one of the batteries of the same regiment as my own. At that time I was able to join his officers in writing to the parents from the front, and I later met some of his family at their home in Norwich, Vermont.[3]

The variety in character and background of our enlisted men in France is well suggested by this scene in our squad room. Though Bartlett was exceptional, the ranks included the bright and the stupid, the skilled and the helpless, the fit and the unfit, the willing and the sullen, the stalwart and the vicious. The officers could depend on the robust intelligence and endurance of most, and prized the initiative and resourcefulness of many. But there were also the laggards, the inept, and the malingerers who had to be carried along as well as those who were assigned to the "brig" or prison detail, if not to the MPs (military police).

In our billet at this time a favorite topic (in addition to the army grub, experiences in passing through Paris, the delays of the mail) was the peculiarities of the French, whom the men always spoke of as the "frogs." Not seldom, it appeared, there had been altercations with French civilians or soldiers in the shops or cafés in the neighborhood. One of our cruder orderlies in the squad room boasted of knocking down a "frog" with his sidecar. But he was put down by another who announced: "That's nothing. I just knocked one down, not with a car or a sidecar but with my G— d—— feet." And he proceeded to cut a notch in a stick he had placed over his bed to keep a record of his assaults on our allies, the "frogs."

That winter I discovered the useful library at the YMCA reading room. The stalemate of the war could continue indefinitely, and I realized that the abridgement of my college studies was extending into a third year. Books on history and social studies were therefore welcome. The ex-soldier—like Napoleon's veterans after Waterloo fixated on their memories, cherished uniforms, and medals—would be like a ghost or alien in the resumed tenor of a world at peace. I wrote home on December 16:

> I doubt not that this winter will be a gloomy one. The world's af-
> fairs are almost irretrievably tangled. It seems more likely that the
> unravelling will be a long blind process than that all should come
> straight with a single pull. There is much evil on both sides and the
> finest utterances of premiers and generals are rather imitations of
> Lincoln, Cromwell, John Bright, etc., than sincere. When one sees
> the seamier side of men, these appeals to them in the name of lib-
> erty, humanity, etc., seem mockery. Whatever there is of wrong on
> the right side will be paid for often by those who had no share in
> it—this is what is meant by redemption.

All such yeasty philosophizing of an adolescent I now recognize as pretentious, but what is inchoate here had its implications and is part of the
record. Another letter adds details about these first days at Valdahon.

> Here's how we spent last Saturday. One of the fellows from
> across the hall banged the door open and bawled half of us awake,
> switched the lights on at 5:45. Sergeant came in and pulled covers
> off H . . . , the tow-headed saddler. Then he let down the head-
> support of R . . . 's bed, the desperado dispatch-rider, though
> he only snoozed on at a 45 degree angle, too mad to remonstrate.
> Sound of long rubber boots being drawn on, and clash of mess-kits.
> The stairs resound and groups hustle through the camp on the hard

snow in the dark. A bustle of tables and of emptying and sending out again of platters. Bacon, toast, molasses syrup, coffee.

Back to barracks. Struggle with stove wood a little wet. Beds made, swept under . . . No water in building, so dash in negligee to empty kitchen to wash. . . . our sergt., little taciturn, low voiced good humored authoritarian fellow, comes in. Says something with a jerk of the head. After mess at noon, another command from the demure [sergeant]. Squad formed at 1:30 with pistols, holsters and belts. We go through saluting, facings, pistol inspection. Excused. . . .

After 5 o'clock mess made toast on stove. The boys discuss the merits of cafes in ———— and in the villages about here; or French drinks, or places to get American food in Paris, or French priests or the girls in the locality, or the advent of pay-day, or the roads or diverse army regulations.

Last night they got snagged on the topic of religion. A fellow about here is prophesying the end of the war in February, based on Revelations xiii, which he expounds with huge superstition. I am astounded at the combination of ignorance and moldy superstition one finds if Christianity is raised in a company like this.

An exceptional officer captained our battery through the critical actions in which the Second Division with its Marines distinguished itself.

Another private, N—— wrote a letter full of obscenity and laid it on a table for Captain R[einhart] to censor [the mandatory safeguard against incautious military disclosure] and send. The Captain called him in and told him it was the dirtiest letter he had ever read; that he would never put his name to that kind of letter, and then gave him a lecture on venereal disease telling of a fellow in the hospital who suffered such agony that when the doctor came in to speak with him he had cried and begged the doctor to shoot him. Captain Stanley Reinhart came from an Ohio farm (near Akron), went to West Point, graduated about 1916. He was a fine military type admired by all the men here. They say he hardly ever says damn.

After the war now Colonel Reinhart was high up if not acting head at

West Point. In the spring of 1920 I was applying for a Rhodes Scholarship, and my overzealous father wired him for a testimonial, no doubt hoping thus to maximize my modest military career which had ended with the rank of corporal. My erstwhile captain replied with a commendatory telegram for the Rhodes committee, pointing out sympathetically in my favor that the kind of abilities in the ranks under his command in the War were those of lumber-jacks, stevedores, and coal-heavers rather than students.

Arrival of the Seventeenth Field Artillery at Valdahon

My affiliation with the headquarters personnel of the camp came to an end with the arrival on January 2, 1918, of the U.S. Seventeenth Field Artillery. I was immediately assigned to A Battery and moved into a different barracks. This regiment, joined by the Twelfth and Fifteenth, eventually made up the artillery brigade of the Second Division which so distinguished itself later at Belleau Wood and Villers-Cotterets.

This brigade had been constituted, after our declaration of war, by expansion of an earlier artillery battalion which had seen service in Mexico and the Philippines. The men had then been in training at Camp Robinson, at Sparta, Wisconsin, until they sailed to Brest in a convoy which arrived at that port on December 27. There they were entrained in the notorious French freight-cars marked 8 CHEVAUX–36 HOMMES, and made the cold journey across France to Valdahon, arriving on January 2.

In this new assignment drills and training now became more systematic. Within eight or ten weeks our batteries would be moving to the front. Experienced French officers joined our staff to help familiarize us with the operation of our French guns. Our regiment, the Seventeenth, with its six batteries, had 155s (155-millimeter howitzers). The Twelfth and Fifteenth regiments had the famous 75s.

In point of matériel, an artillery regiment in the field required not only guns—in their emplacements—but also ammunition, constantly replenished, and instruments, maps, and supplies of various kinds. All this had to be mobile, and before motorization (which for us came after the Armistice) each battery had its horses a mile or more behind its more exposed position. On the road all this took the form of a lengthy file of guns and caissons, each pulled by yoked horses, and of wagons, with mounted officers accompanying the gun crews and other men following on foot.

When the camouflaged guns were in firing position in a given sector, orders would come by field telephone or courier from the colonel at regimental headquarters to our captain. So many rounds of either explosive or shrapnel shells at such and such times and with such and such frequency. The targets were identified by coordinates on a grid map of the area which showed its features in great detail. Using the map our officers could determine the direction and distance of the target in relation to our position. Allowance had to be made, however, for such factors as atmospheric conditions as well as distortion in the maps themselves.

Trial firings by our guns therefore needed to be observed from a forward position. Our telephone detail would string wires through the woods and fields to such an observation post. Instructing our gunners to fire, the officer could then note how far the shot was "over" or "short," right or left, and thus correct the following trial. This was known as "controlling fire." Once a correction was established for this position of the battery it could be incorporated in any further targetings there.

Our howitzers were usually at some distance behind the front lines. The looping trajectory of their shells had a range of up to twelve miles.* The targets included not only the enemy trench systems but also batteries, crossroads, and assembly points in their rear.

The shells of our 155-millimeter (approximately 6-inch) guns weighed over 90 pounds. These were brought in at night so that traffic in and out of our hidden battery location would not help enemy planes spot our position. Even worn tracks off a road into a copse could arouse suspi-

---

*Amos Wilder had planned, but was not able before his death to double check this figure and the following description of how a 155-millimeter gun was fired. The actual range was about seven miles, not twelve. In the description of how the gun was fired, "direction" and "trajectory" should read "azimuth" and "elevation," each routine requiring a separate man. It took two men to ram home the shell after two others had screwed on its fuse and carried the shell by tray to the breech. Finally, another man added the primer and closed the breech-block, and pulled the lanyard.

cion. After delivery the shells were laid in tiers just below the surface of the ground for greater security, just as were our sleeping blankets that served as beds. With the shells came also bags of powder and fuses. When a gun was fired one member of the gun crew adjusted the barrel for the required direction and trajectory; another rammed home the shell after screwing on its fuse; another added the powder charge (a bag not actually of powder but of thin yellow strips); a fourth closed the breech-block; then all seven of the gun crew put their fingers in their ears as the last, at the officer's command, pulled the lanyard.

All had cotton in their ears, especially this last whose hands were not free thus to dull the deafening discharge. In my early experiences with A Battery at Valdahon, I was with a squad having its first live drill on the guns. No one had remembered to bring cotton to the exercises. So when it came to pulling the lanyard it fell to me because I was wearing a wool helmet on that freezing day, but the covering of my ears did little to shield me from the impact of the detonation.

I wrote home on January 10 telling of my move to A Battery and the new regime into which I was thus initiated. I now had a spring bed in a large room accommodating twenty-six men.

Today my first training began at 5:30. Ten minutes later there was assembly in the dark and a howling blizzard outside [non-coms using flashlights to read off the names at the roll-call]. This roll-call was followed by breakfast. Everybody tried to get to the head of the endless line waiting to go through the kitchen with open mess-kits. Then they line up again for "seconds" before the "firsts" are through. For breakfast we had steak and rich gravy. Our battery has no horses yet so there is no stables detail.

At 7 assembly again. Several gun crews go out to their pieces and the instruction. The first sergeant says to a non-com, "Take the rest out for a hike until 9." We break out our own trail in single file through snow a foot deep at the shallowest places and return through the blinding snow glowing after a few short rests on the way. "Take 'em out for a little walk until 11," comes next after a bit of snow-shoveling. The walking is hard labor but it is a godsend against the cold. Besides, our room has been denied a fire all day because there had been fuel hoarding on the sly there. At 11, in spite of walking, my feet were still cold. I only got them warm again when we were sent out walking for the third time at 3 p.m. By this time the atmosphere was getting heavier and the snow packed. We had a snow fight for a while. For some of this bunch, who are recruits of a few months standing, the work is very laborious; but our morale was brought up to O.K. by the scuffle. They seem to be regular kids—some are little fellows and all are young. The older ones are in the gun crews. We get that training later, I guess . . . .

Since I wrote the above we have had retreat and I am in the warm, lighted YMCA hut and will probably stay here in spite of the attractions (films, music, boxing) in the Auditorium next door. I have been doing daily work on French idioms, and besides Goethe's *Faust* have been reading *Récits d'un soldat* about the war of 1870.

Tom Haslitt [Australian, formerly Dascomb House chaplain, Oberlin] writes me from his Battery in the hottest part of the British front for the last six months.

I'm ready to spend another winter over here if need be. Uncle Sam's wardrobe and accommodations make this cold weather nothing at all compared with those first weeks in the Argonne last February. [During my service with Section 2 of the American Field Service, we were housed in rooms or in excavated *abris;* the lower temperatures that winter involved more exposure to chill and frost-bite for the ambulance drivers.]

I am rather sorry to see the prevalence of the idea that peace is immediately at hand. The soldiers with considerable interest talk of all kinds of vague rumors. The Russo-German armistice is supposed to include the United States, etc. I'm glad that with my 15 months experience I can be here at the base of things (a private) and help a little in the creating of the right war-attitude among the men. One has to take the side of the French often, too, for many of the American soldiers fail completely to understand them. They call them "frogs," from "frog-eaters," and with real dislike. American privates just arrived cannot remember that France lost many of the best it had in 1914, let alone the last three years. They only see the lack of abundance and other things that are different from home, most of them as a result of the ravages of war.

"A" Battery, Jan. 18

President Wilson's Peace Terms are out today. If the Germans accept them I shall be much surprised. I think the French will be taken aback at our saying nothing of monetary reparation. They have got the American giant jumping about in the ring perfectly up to now and they will be stricken to tears if he proceeds to take the direction of things into his own hands. If President Wilson can save the nation the "Spring's Baptism of Fire" he will deserve the thanks of the American people.

January 20

I would be pleased to see the Russians repudiate the German imperialists, with whom they treat so precariously, terminate the armistice, and appeal to the German Socialists to help them war against Russia again. The French papers anticipate a big German offensive one of these days—whether it will come off or not depends on how much the Germans fear the advent of America.

At this time both the Central Powers and the Allies were still unsure as to the effectiveness of the role America could play in this distant theatre of operations. Much, indeed, was heard of the astonishing "war effort" at home, the mobilization, the coordination of industry and labor, the taking over of the railroads, and so on. But all this was looked on with a degree of skepticism, and this weakened the force of President Wilson's overtures to peace with his Fourteen Points. The lofty Kaiser and his entourage exhibited here the same myopia as with regard to other peoples and their motivations. They were, however, soon to be confronted by massive military and moral reinforcements of the Allies from the New World.

The fact is that there were unaccountable factors on both sides in the calculus of this global war from the beginning. Apart from the repercussions in the Balkans, the Middle East, and the colonies of the warring

European powers, who could have predicted the Russian Revolution and the collapse of that front or the events which brought American forces on the scene? Deeper than all these were conflicting issues and motivations affecting the morale of the combatants such as surfaced in the mutiny of French units in 1917 and the fateful demoralization of the Hapsburg regime and the Austrian army in 1918. Such fissures and instabilities lay behind the fierce and recurrent strife amid and between the British and the French over strategy just as they were only partially resolved in the American public and "Woodrow Wilson's war." The Hohenzollern sway in Germany had eventually to come to terms with the equally rooted and sounder legacies of Bavaria, Baden, Hesse, Württemburg, and so on. Prussia retained its grip as long as it did because of the inbred submission to rulers or princes which went back to the time of Luther.

All these latent rifts and divided counsels affected the course of the war and emerged fatefully in the Versailles peace negotiations and their sequel. During the ordeal the obedience of the soldiery even in such an unschooled levy as that of my battery was coupled with vocal opinions about such topics as "war aims," world policing, and democracy. One also heard the usual diatribes against pacifists, slackers, and profiteers on the home front as well as imprecations against the enemy as Huns and perpetrators of atrocities.

"A" Battery, 17 F.A.
Jan. 27, 28

At 7 "assembly" is blown and the two whistles bring us out. Arrived at attention the "old man" (first sergeant) says, "First two gun squads, fall out." Then, "Secondary gun squads, fall out." "Take the rest of these men on a hike" or "for rifle practice." We on the gun squads go to our pieces and "prepare for action." "Into battery, halt." And we do the bits of work assigned to our respective positions. I, at No. 3, stand behind the caisson, prepare the charges by removing from the powder bags one or two or three of the five bundles of powder strips. Also I screw the fuses on the shell and call off the rounds fired in a manner "brutally plain." After a while of dummy practice (we may fire on the range soon) we go to rifle drill and calisthenics.

Today, Saturday, is a half-holiday. In the afternoon there was inspection, and the long awaited pay was given out. I got a pass and went downtown to get my laundry.

. . . I take a real satisfaction in seeing this training approach its completion because I want America to help France immediately in case a death struggle should take place during the winter or in the spring as expected . . . At the same time I remember the mutual uncomfortableness—mental anguish—of Ambulance experience and realize well what it will mean to be out again. We had an "Alert" here the other night and old sensations were revived at the thought of German planes overhead. The amusing thing, however, is that momentary mental anguish of the worst kind has no permanent results. As soon as one's ambulance had turned a corner or the shells concentrate on a new point, it was as though it had never happened. Like the dentist's.

Another thought about the fear of battle. There is a great anesthesia to danger in the common risk. Dashing into position with a battery, the intricate moves and absorption in tasks for which one has been trained, all this dull one's individual anxiety. Just so a man in violent action is not aware for a time that he has been hit and wounded. It was different with the solitary ambulance driver. On a shelled road he could feel as though he were the only target in France!

This letter continues with details about two other assignments. In one, a signal detail with binoculars and mapping instruments was taken to an eminence overlooking the firing range. We were instructed in sketching panoramic maps, presumably of hostile territory, and in using the detailed military charts for the orientation of fire. More arduous was guard duty with armed watch and patrolling of various areas and properties on a fixed rotation, which included postings late at night. With this went instruction about challenges and passwords. To stand guard from midnight to three under the stars in this remote landscape was an uncanny experience. In the silence one could imagine one heard the sound of an avalanche in the Alps to the east and, to the north, the vibrations of gunfire in the heights of the Vosges.

Later, as a student living in Divinity Hall at Harvard, I met an Englishman named Denman who had been a "Tommy" during the war. On one occasion he had been on guard in an advanced *sap* (a covered trench) at night near the junction of a trench manned by another company which might have been infiltrated by enemy spies or saboteurs. Hearing approaching footsteps he called on the invisible figure once and then again to halt and identify himself. The intruder still coming on, Denman finally shot and then found that he had killed a deaf French officer! He was later exonerated by a court-martial. Denman, who later served the Unitarian parish in Harvard, Massachusetts, never showed signs of any particular trauma following this episode in line of duty.

As an artilleryman my ordeal throughout had little in common with that of the infantry and others involved in the atrocious aspects of the trenches and hand-to-hand conflict. Yet the confraternity of arms under the red and baleful eye of Mars has its pervasive solidarity. Those of us who served with long-range guns of course never confronted the enemy directly. Our dueling was like blindman's buff, and we saw neither those who shelled us nor the victims of our fire. The actualities of battle, if not its desperation and exhaustion, were thus depersonalized for us. Our solicitude was for the exposed units in the trenches or the open that our salvos or drumfire sought to protect. What afterthoughts we may have had appealed not only to the line of duty but to the task of order in a disordered world.

This general question of public and, indeed, international order and its necessary authority and compulsions—the whole issue of force in human society—had its microcosm in the handling of insubordination in our batteries. One guard duty I never happened to share was that of the prison detail. As in all human or all-too-human affairs, our officers had to deal with the disorderly, the heedless, the inept, the malcontent. This disruptive element could not be discharged or sent home. The self-willed and the laggards—as in the wider world-scheme—had to be coerced, brought into line, compelled to "shape up," as the army jargon put it.

In a letter home I described the handling of those in the guard house of our regiment.

They get up at an earlier hour than the rest of the camp and are taken down to the bath-house for a shower, warm at first, and then cold. Then they have "double-time" and calisthenics [still in the dark,] and are assigned to road-making, etc., for the rest of the day. The officer in charge of them [Lt. Ratajczak, always called "Rattle-jack"] is a character—famous as a disciplinarian and "rider," that is, he "rides" his men. Many have sworn to kill him when they "get out," (of the army). I heard him talk to them yesterday. He told them they were just weights on the back of the army and worse than Germans, and then proceeded to insult and drill them relentlessly. He always does what they do, however—cold showers, running and all of it. It's the only way to treat men who haven't the yoke in their homes, and there are few who buck any length of time against him.

I can add that it was not uncommon for his initiates later to boast of having gone through his mill. In later actions when the division was subjected to violent shelling including a gas attack Lt. Ratajczak was one of the officers who was awarded a Croix de guerre by the French under whom we were serving in April 1918.

During this period I was assigned to various duties. One day I was acting as orderly in the battery office, about the time I was promoted to the rank of corporal. With some other non-coms, especially when I was on the signal detail, I received a single mount after the horses of the regiment arrived. The trouble was that our calisthenics for this personnel now took the form of bareback tag. The others already had the best of the excitable horses from their Wisconsin training period. Though I had had a lot of riding at the Thacher School in California, my nag was both slow and razorback, and after I was tagged it was therefore hard to catch anyone.

One entry in my diary tells of a Protestant service one Sunday night.

Major [Maynard] of 1st Batl. 17th, led the singing and then gave an impassioned extempore [sermon] on the "Prussians" in our own outfits he had seen [misbehaving] in Valdahon, etc. Then Captain [Reinhart], the ballistics expert gave a talk on "manly prayer."

As proof of God he told of being up 3000 feet in an aeroplane the other day and seeing the whole Alps in the sunset glow, also the Vosges, the lines, and the Black Forest with the effects of cloud, wind, rain and scattered snow.

The rigors of our training in this period are suggested by an entry in my journal from Saturday, January 12:

Inspection in morning. First bunk inspection (with field equipment) by Battery officer, Lt. Davis. Then, outside, inspection of hat, overcoat, uniform, and boots by Major M[aynard], who held us at attention in the cold so long that it was a torture. Besides that, I had my feet jammed into boots much too small for me and they had been freezing an hour before and during preliminaries. After a half hour at attention outdoors I had involuntary tremors, then began to get dizzy. Just as it came to a crisis I left ranks, which I probably should not have done, but I would have hit the ground the next minute. I did not feel well until changing to my big roomy shoes and getting a hot dinner. Besides me one other fellow threw up in ranks and two others were sick.

I could appreciate, however, the significance of all these rituals and drills in our training. By such repeated protocols the claims of authority and hierarchy become second nature to the soldier in preparation for what must be unquestioning and concerted response under extreme demands. This explains the exaggerated style of some military traditions in which the regimented have taken on the character of automatons, as in the case of the Nazi goose step or the decorum of the samurai. Some great vocations have thus been fashioned out of malleable human material by initiations, ordeals, abstinences, and shaping regimes, whether one thinks of the Spartans or the monastic orders of the Church. The whole topic raises interesting questions with regard to modern ideas of individual autonomy and personal or group "rights."

One had to serve only a short time in a regiment like ours, however, to realize that surprising individual talents and spontaneity were not submerged in any dull brainwashed uniformity. One instance of such unexpected resourcefulness occurred during a program put on for the men in the YMCA hall. Two entertainers were performing, no doubt making the rounds of the camps. (In our pre-Bob Hope days such celebrities as Harry Lauder and Elsie Janis were favorites.)

> Mr. and Mrs. Rogers read to us, gave recitations and led in the singing. Henley's "Invictus" went fine. An amusing incident when above the weak general singing of some popular song rose a stentorian tenor from right under the stage, just on the last notes. Everybody roared, and Mr. Rogers was both nettled and pleased. Why wouldn't [our unknown Caruso] sing like that all the time? But no; in succeeding songs only at the end and sometimes not then.

The regiment congratulated itself that it included a recruit from the Metropolitan Opera! Another notable I had encountered was our cook in Section 2 in the American Field Service, who had been chef at the Café de la Paix in Paris.

My account of the entertainment concludes as follows:

> Mr. Rogers sang "The Rosary," saying that Ethelbert Nevin had written it *for him* when they were students together in Paris twenty years ago.

In retrospect this interests me because our later summer home at Blue Hill Falls in Maine was close by the beautiful villa of Nevin's widow. The villa, called "Arcady," was commonly spoken of as "the House that 'The Rosary' built."

On Saturday, February 9, I had been able to foregather with some Yale contemporaries who were in the Seventeenth Regiment or in our brigade at Valdahon.

> Dinner leave with Charlie Taft (Sgt.-Major, 12th Regiment), Thomas (Sgt., squad detail, A Battery, 12th), both Yale '18; Meredith (Sgt. in charge A detail, 12th), Allen (Sgt., gun squad, 12th; football star, Yale '18), Stackpole, Yale '19 (of Brigade Hdqtrs.); also Wharton, Harvard '17.

These students had left their college studies and had already worked their way into the ranks, no doubt with some military training but without the full ROTC course which would have delayed their participation.

My journal entries for the first days of March indicate that our training at Valdahon was drawing to a close. The history of the regiment states that the last "problem" was fired on the range on March 8. A field drill with the horses and guns on the road was carried out. In the long file of several batteries I was deputed as agent for A Battery, on horseback. I had to communicate orders, sometimes at a gallop, between Captain Reinhart and Major Maynard, commander of our First Battalion.

From Valdahon to the Front

At this point I quote the regimental history:

The Brigade was ready and impatient to go to the front. It was known that the 12th, 15th and 17th would comprise the Second F. A. Brigade, which would be a part of the American Second Division. This division was to go into a quiet sector under the command and direction of the French, which proved to be in the vicinity of Rupt, on the line south of Verdun. The Regiment entrained at Besançon in six sections, leaving at intervals of four hours.

Our battery left Valdahon at midnight, the officers moving about with flashlights. In my journal I recorded the excitement of the men.

The four pieces and their caissons went first, then us, the detail mounted, then the supply wagons (carrying also our barrack bags) and the kitchen wagon, smoking. One felt something of a thrill as we hit the main road for Besançon—24 miles away—the camp shut and sleeping behind us. For we were the first of the Brigade to leave.

A great ride— that to Besançon. The hourly stops—the officers riding up and down—the occasional scenes with a refractory horse—the passing up and down of the sung-out orders "Cannoneers, Halt." "Prepare to dismount." "Dismount." The half-a-mile of convoy—hoofbeats, grating of wheels and brakes.

The thought that at last one had found the army of all ages and lands of young men going forth to war.

The sky got lighter and we could make out the teams pulling the caisson ahead of us and identify the men who had been nodding (precariously) on it. Then it got real light and we saw the road begin to descend steeply from the Jura level to the plain and the river Doubs. A somewhat proud passage through the old town (our banner staff up but the banner rolled). Watering horses, loading pieces, wagons and horses on flat and box cars. First meal at 12 noon. Then 22 of us in box car with all our equipment except saddles. Anti-aircraft shrapnel overhead as we left town [directed at enemy observers this far in the rear].

There were complex problems of logistics and organization involved in moving battery, battalion, regiment, brigade to the lines; schedules of detraining, available billeting from stage to stage as we moved toward our destination, the timing of our replacement of the departing French artillery which had occupied our positions—all this in the exposed *zone des Armées*, and in a foreign land with the consequent problems of liaison and synchronization. In this period in which rain was sometimes unrelenting, meals were irregular, and we would have to resort to our emergency rations, "corn-wooly," and so on. But a perennially harrassing vexation for the artillery was our horses. They had to have their nosebags and be led to water twice a day, and on occasion the only troughs or *abreuvoirs* were a kilometer distant from our bivouacs. Add to these demands the sheer weight of our guns on inclines and on bombed, deteriorated, and washed-out roads.

By Thursday, March 21, we were some miles south of Verdun preparing to move east across the Meuse and to march after dark to our designated positions in the Rupt sector, more specifically to Les Eparges. The men had been excited by our increasing proximity to the front, by the glamour of such names as Verdun and the Meuse, and cheered by the improvement of the weather. In my journal I noted:

Last night the cannoneers went up to the emplacements in trucks. The rest of us go tonight. Checking up of horses and equipment.

At 6 the column moves again and another battery takes our place immediately. "A" Battery is the first American artillery to go into position in the region.

I am called for—"Corporal Wilder, ride up with the guide." A French lieutenant. He tells me to ride beside him, and his orderly falls back. We pace out toward the country, ahead of the one-third mile train. A clear starry night with a half moon. Down through the woods, and then a steep [town?], shelled to pieces, where Americans are now in reserve cantonments. The Lt. says we are fortunate in that no German aeroplanes had been over who might report our approach. No firing to be heard except north towards Verdun. The American officers B———— and Lt. ————, worrying some about the interval between pieces.

We make the crossing over the river [the Meuse] and canal by a long causeway. A very memorable ride. Hills and picturesque terrain and a sense of adventure. One wondered about the sensations of the Battery—those who had never been to the front.

So we went up to Rupt, where the combat and field trains separated, the former going on to the gun emplacements, and the latter to the billets [near Rupt]. I was sent as guide-interpreter with the latter.

This factual account of our crossing of the Meuse, written at the time, can be set against a more imaginative recital in a poem which I wrote in 1928, "Ten Years Ago, March 21, 1918."[4] The scenario is the same, but the mythic dimension of verse evokes more vividly the overtones of the experience as they were obscurely felt by all in the advancing column. The one additional feature of this record is the stunning passage overhead of the Allied bombing squadrons. This episode, though absent from my journal, must have been factual since I recalled it so graphically.

. . . The moon was bright, the night was still—and there
The Hills of Death with their sepulchral stare.
Somnolent, ominous, with now a blunt
Report that told no tales, we sensed the Front,
. . . The Front, that fatal River, by whose verge

Millions wrought, frantic lest the world submerge.
Our guns and caissons thundered on the bridge,
No lightning answered from the Woëvre ridge.
The Meuse amid its sedges dreamed too deep
In Moonlight to be startled from its sleep.
Its gilded waters had their life too far
In ancient nature to remark our war.
Our echoes died upon the loosened timbers,
We climbed the Right Bank with our heavy limbers,
And passed in clamor, under the Great Wain,
One of the calcined Cities of the Plain.
We left the River and we left the marsh
And felt the grade which leads to Les Eparges.
The night was still, a desultory thunder
Far in the west hardly aroused our wonder.
But then an undertone grew to a hum,
We heard the Allied bombing squadrons come.
The hum grew to a mighty pulse, and soon
The midnight was a-throb beneath the moon.
The deafening revolutions stunned our ears
As though we heard the gyrations of the spheres.
The moon was bright; we saw their silhouettes
Pass o'er its face upon their way to Metz:
The insects floated o'er the argent disk
Ten thousand miles from earth—beyond all risk,
Safe in the world of myth, and led us too
Into the apotheosis they knew.
For silence fell upon the toiling line,
The shadowy convoy recognized the sign.
A stupor seized the long nocturnal train,
Guide, staff, interpreter alike drew rein.
Driver and cannoneer gestured above,
Almost the regiment forgot to move.
Across the zenith passed the fabulous throng,
The whole concave of heaven rang like a gong.

79

✳

March
1918

Castor and Pollux at Lake Regulus!
But Prodigy had likewise greeted us
And we went into battle under omens
Like all before, Trojans and Greeks and Romans. . . .

The poem concludes even more mythologically, or as some might say, grandiloquently. My longer and more ambitious poem "Armageddon" deals with the crucial battle at the Forêt de Villers-Cotterets in July. Over against the objections of those who demur at what they see as romanticizing of war I would defend, not the poems themselves, but the imaginative registers in terms of which such momentous transactions are felt. Human experience is not one-dimensional, and the deeper import of even less dramatic actions calls across time and space for answering voices. For me, this episode really happened in a way which imposed itself on my later visionary transcription. The toiling line of the whole brigade likewise had its inklings of that transposed reality which the poetic version alone could seek to articulate.

When I arrived as interpreter with the field train at Rupt, it was a question of the location and billeting of all those elements of an artillery unit not in the more advanced position of the guns and the combat personnel. My function was as intermediary with the local French supervisors of the encampment and its accommodations.

> The *casernier* told me where everything was—stables, officers' stables, veterinarian stable, barracks, police post, officers' quarters, non-com barracks, forge, infirmary. The Frenchmen thought the officers would want first of all to know where their own quarters were and let the men take care of themselves. The officers insisted on seeing the men located and horses fed. I heard one Frenchman say to another, "They pay much more attention to their men than ours [officers]."

The location was six miles from the front and had not been subjected to bombing. At night all lights were forbidden.

In the Rupt-en-Woëvre Sector, March 21 to May 14

Our regimental history summarizes this period as follows:

> Positions were quickly taken. The Regiment was the first artillery in
> the Division to throw shells over the line. The Regiment familiarized
> itself in the different kinds of fire, such as—fire for destruction,
> harrassing fire, counter-battery, counter-offensive, and participation
> in coups-de-main . . .
>
> On March 31 there was a successful coup-de-main under General
> Boyer with whom the Second Division was working. On April 16
> the press had a report of extremely heavy shelling by the American
> heavy artillery, which silenced two enemy batteries.
>
> During the stay in this sector the batteries were at times subjected
> to violent shelling . . . Battery "C" received a shower of gas shells.

During this period our A Battery was well concealed in a wooded
gorge in the hills. The only near explosion I recall was one of our own
shells overhead as it encountered high branches of a neighboring tree.

After the billeting operations I was assigned to the instrument detail
at our forward position with the guns. Our first days on the firing line
were strangely calm, as I noted in my journal:

> The Battery in reserve position—no firing [i.e., by our pre-
> decessors] in months. American Marines and French units in
> cantonments about us. The pieces camouflaged and surrounded
> with dug-outs for the gun crews and details, with kitchen a little
> way off in the ravine. German plane over us at night and shrapnel
> on the roads always in the early morning, but in general everybody
> disappointed with the tameness of it. They laugh at the Frenchmen
> who advise us not to fire because the Germans will retaliate on the
> camps near the Battery. Some doubt if we will fire at all.

The past had its role in our new location. In addition to news of a German attack in the west, our crew stringing telephone wires to connect
the battery with Battalion Headquarters found old wire entanglements
in the woods that dated back to September 1914.

At 10:30 Sgt. Vencill, Cpl. Glorvigen and self sent for to go with Captain Reinhart and Lt. Richardson to observation post with instruments to direct Battery's first fire. The officers set out at a fearful pace, and Captain Reinhart was crazy to fire. He couldn't get up there quick enough, and he couldn't wait until 1 P.M. but at 12:59 told them to let it go, "A" Battery's first against the Germans—the object of all our work till then and its justification. From our small box in the trees overlooking a ravine of trenches we could see enemy land and the front trenches of both sides. It was a mere jump across to our objective, I suppose 1/2 mile in an air line to the Germans. But their trenches were deserted and we only "regulated" on an intersection for a barrage index.

The officers were very gay through it all . . . They took 100 shells to lay all four guns on the point. Several were "target," etc. Every so often we would hear from the Battery that there were German machines overhead, or that some gun was withdrawn for cleaning or had misfired, and there would be a wait. I recorded as usual: deflection, rounds, elevation, sensing . . .

It was interesting to hear the officers talk in between whiles. Our old friend Major, M[aynard], was called the "jug-head," and there were some dirty stories. Also talk about the German progress on the big attack.

We went back (nothing to eat since breakfast, of course) at 4:30 past the rear trenches, dug-outs and billets. Some in the French billets eye us askance. They have been living on indulgent terms with the Boche for some time. Their artillery had been well enough trained not to irritate the enemy. Now comes the American with his aggressive tactics and stirs up the hornets' nest so that they have to live within two steps of shelters, gas masks and helmets. A French soldier said, "C'est un secteur trés tranquil—trés, trés tranquil—il faut pas l'abîmer!" Their officers and men urge the policy of live-and-let-live where possible. The Americans do not yet understand this, not knowing what life in a hot sector is and how welcome a quiet sector is, for a rest.

One memory of these weeks is still vivid with me. I accompanied Lt. Richardson, both of us mounted, to a different observation point overlooking the area of our battery fire. Soon we found ourselves pacing south on a long high ridge where our road was concealed from the enemy on the east by a continuous high curtain of baize or canvas, camouflaged by paint so as to blend into the woods to the west. After a time we left our horses, and with our binoculars and instruments went on to a lookout which we hoped had not become suspect by the Germans. Our view here commanded the enemy lines below and the country eastward included in the *so-called* St.-Mihiel salient.

Here we had field telephone connections with our battery and were able to direct and control fire on designated targets. On our way back while still on foot we were alerted to gas in the area by seeing others with their gas masks on, though we had not heard the usual warning klaxons. We hastily put on our masks and stumbled back to our mounts where we felt safe in removing them.

At the end of March and in early April there was periodic shelling of our area. "*Minnewerfers* [mortars] and shells about in second lines," reads a note I made at the time. "The billets near us shelled by Boches. Two French killed and some wounded." Going over to battalion headquarters Captain Reinhart and others found a crossroad being shelled. They saw a shell kill two horses and leave four men immediately behind them unharmed.

During the night the 75s (of the Twelfth or Fifteenth Regiments) were firing, and we had been laid to fire.

> We in the telephone dug-out were awake a good part of the time, waiting for and listening to the *arrivés* [incoming shells] on near-by batteries and crossroads. We all had our masks for 15 minutes about 2 A.M. gas being reported. One of the batteries got 500 gas shells and no casualties. They kept on firing a barrage with masks on.

Wed. April 3

Last night at 2:30 fired a few rounds and then ordered to cease by Col. Bowley. Today we regulated by a point of reference [on our map and enemy battery, the observing being done for us by a French balloon high above us]. They say there is an American 16″ naval gun back here on a railroad [flatcar] about to fire.

One episode of this period in a quiet sector reflects its lighter moments and the ebullience of the men. A German shell exploded in the trees close by our rolling kitchen, which was a little way off in the ravine. The hit was close enough so that our chef and his crew felt the immediate blast of air, while scatterings of leaves and debris threatened to get into their pots and pans. Our cook, Mike, was a character and very popular with everybody, and this intrusion on him and his KP's (kitchen police) as they busied themselves with their cauldrons of soup, and so on, vastly amused the boys, who could not stop laughing at his surprise. One wag coined the appropriate order for their predicament: "Chow-detail, Attention! Present ladles! To the rear! March!"

I shall now confine myself to selected notations, made necessary due to the deteriorated condition of my journal. At this point the pages of my small notebook are falling out and my jottings of seventy-three years ago are increasingly illegible.

The hilarity of the boys over the discomfiture of our kitchen crew, despite the overhanging cloud of war—under the volcano—may suggest long-thought-about human obliviousness generally. But it could later translate itself into the bravado and resilience of the troops in more perilous ordeals. One recalls the taunt with which the sergeant spurred on his platoon: "Come on, you b—— , do you want to live forever!"

But there was another aspect of morale at the front, reported in my journal entry for April 3:

A very intelligent French infantryman from Manitoba [*sic*] was in our dug-out last night. He spoke very comically of his experience in, and dislike for, New York elevators. The second time he visited the French consul he walked up the 21 flights. He was discouraged about the prospect of achieving a desirable peace, and said most of the French soldiers would be satisfied to leave things as they were before 1914. No use in taking [back] Alsace-Lorraine; not worth it. Germany has had them for 45 years; let her keep them. The French soldiers will not fight after this fall. The only reason they are fighting this year is that they thought it worth while to see what America could do.—One meets these attitudes of compromise among the French.—He admitted that peace must bring a democratic and disarmed Germany, though.

One may find in this passing momentary candor of a veteran of the trenches an index of the turmoil of motivations in the fourth year of excruciating travail. The scourge of war had penetrated to the souls of all the peoples involved to the extent that even such a pillar of French nationalism as the bond with Alsace and Lorraine, the lost provinces, had been undermined. Yet there persisted Europe's ingrained aspiration toward a just order for whose accomplishment they now looked wistfully to the New World.

The amusing dismay with New York's elevators is also revealing in its own way. That succession of French writers who visited the United States and shaped the European image of our soulless and materialist civilization—carried over into Kafka's *Amerika*—loved to dwell on the impersonality of our skyscrapers as symbols of empty power. The Frenchman with his parochial pieties either of the village or the boulevards and their palaces and gardens could not find his way in our engineering marvels or recognize the cultural values of our way of life. This disparagement of our philistinism had much to do with our Franco-American associations in the war and in the sequel.

After noting the activities of the Marines of our division in our area I observed in my journal that

all American soldiers I have seen so far are boys—insouciance, garrulousness, belligerency, prejudice, naiveté, enthusiasm and pliability. A little unreliable and slippery for the officers, but it would take a long time to sour them.

I also recorded the location of our telephone and instrument details.

Our dug-out is about 10 yards from the first piece, a descending 1 ½ foot wide trench leading into it. [It is] a 10 ft wider trench, 25 feet long, into which one stumbles, arched over with heavy corrugated iron. A two-layer framework holds chicken-wire beds for

4 above and 4 below in pairs lengthwise, with a table near entrance for telephone. Rain seeps through sidewalls and makes a canal of the little passageway along the side of the bunks. . . .

Walker and I sleep on adjoining bunks with our blankets and shelter-tent halves for cover, and other men above us. Coats, mess kits, masks, helmets, slickers, barracks-bags and saddle-bags are on the earth floor or hung on the bed frames.

I made a lamp out of a baking-powder can and cartridge with cotton and kerosene. A bit of coal oil gives me a light for 6 or 8 hours.

I had learned this trick from the French when I was in the ambulance service. In those days in Macedonia and on the French front one found poilus who in their spare time were ingenious in fashioning souvenirs, especially *briquets* (lighters), out of empty cartridges or copper from shell-casings—just as sailors amuse themselves with whittling miniature ships.

Each [gun] section has a dug-out, camouflaged, near its piece. The chiefs-of-section are together and boast of their "dog-robbers" [orderlies], and of not coming to our [common] mess for days at a time almost in view of their own culinary arrangements.

The leaders of the several gun crews boasted a prestige that fell between that of a "non-com" and an officer. Even in this situation one sees that touch of envy which hierarchy always occasions.

Wed. 10th April

Shells from Deutschland yesterday 1 P.M. to 12 midnight and today from 6 A.M. to 1—every 10 to 15 or 30 minutes. Business goes on as usual but gets on one's nerves. Nobody hit but barracks punctured and several (myself included) covered with stones and dust. Rotten shells—77s and 105s but many do not explode in mud, and the ammunition and brass in them show Germans' shortage. Kitchen goes on right in the midst of it. We are digging an incline tunnel from our dug-out, for as a Frenchman said, its iron-sheeting roof is good for keeping the sun out.

Wagner chosen by chance and lot to go home for Liberty Loan promotion. Apparently our 250 rounds the other day destroyed or dislodged a battery which has never since spoken but was daily loquacious before.

I combine a short account in my journal of April 21 and a long one in a letter home of May 5 reporting:

Best Sunday sermon I ever hope to have—[At a long meeting] Cap't Reinhart [aware of my earlier interest in a commission, AFS service and Croix de guerre] says I am lacking in aggressiveness—men in ranks may go for commission but B.C [battalion commander] cannot recommend a man unless he has shown he can work with men. Says he will give me a trial with details . . . Scared me to death. Asked me about college training—mathematics and business.

The secret of handling men and getting jobs done by a bunch of them is an exhibition of energy on your own part. It's contagious. But you've got to make an effort. You have to expend energy. Now I'm going to let 1st Lieut. ——— give you some details "to take out and see what you can do. I want you to develop this ability to handle men."

Well, the first detail I had was that night. I was scared sick. I didn't know what I'd do if one of them "laid down" on me—whether I'd threaten to lick him physically or just weakly report him. I was nauseated with the whole thing. But we have such a good top sergeant that it went off well enough. The mere momentum of the daily work carried the men through it with a little joking stimulus from me. Other times haven't gone so well.

Though I was not all that ambitious to be an officer (and there were many in our battalion ahead of me for such promotion) this searching little sermon no doubt left its mark on my later demeanor as an academic, many of whom shield themselves from the practical and morale-building aspects of life in the educational community.

The transition of our battery to a new theater of action is summarized as follows in our regimental history.

Rupt, Vannault-les-Dames, Chambord

After its stay in a quiet sector at the front, the Division was due for organization as an independent unit. On May 14, the Regiment was on the move. The guns had been taken out and our positions taken over by the French. After a march of three days the Regiment reached Vannault-les-Dames, between Bar-le-Duc and Vitry. In three more days the Regiment entrained at Revigny. There followed detraining and a march to Chambord, between Paris and Rouen. Here the Division was organized as an American Division and a problem was worked on May 27. The Infantry of the Division consisted of the 9th and 23rd Infantry and the 5th and 6th Marines. The machine gun battalions were the 4th and 5th. June 1 found the 17th F. A., after participating in Divisional Maneuvers, in the vicinity of Lattainville in the act of moving.

This complicated itinerary took us to the neighborhood of Meaux, not far northeast of Paris. The purpose, especially in later shifts, was to position us for the expected German drive which eventuated in the engagements in and about Château-Thierry and the Second Battle of the Marne. For me this shuttling to and fro among French villages and railheads in the rear meant a far more attractive assignment, that of local billeting, a role for which my familiarity with French qualified me. Shortly before the battery decamped from the Rupt sector, I wrote:

[From a letter home of May 12]
[One of our lieutenants] came up to our dug-out and called for me. "How'd you like to go on a little party with me?" he said with a small smile.

"Great dope, lieutenant."

"All right. Pack up all your equipment and be ready in 15 minutes." (Exit)

So it was off that night to headquarters and a chance to see a movie show; great treat; and the next day way off—any number of kilometers from the Battery. You can't even hear any guns here. A group of us non-coms are living here temporarily, and the lieutenants give us work to do. We have so many day's rations from the Bat-

tery—cold army beef, bacon and hard tack. But there is the most
obliging lady below—talks about our coming to defend her country,
and warms and cooks whatever we have: bacon, eggs, chocolate.

I have the best visits with the family. The father is a government
road supervisor. There is the wife, a daughter of 20 or so and a boy
of 10. These people are evacuees from Rheims . . . The daughter
sends the enclosed lily of the valley to one of my sisters . . .

May 19

Since writing last I have been back with the Battery and then
again separated on special duty—and a thousand different experiences and incidents, mostly of a pacific nature. Lots and lots of talk
with French people, seeing all kinds of troops, villages and farms.

My letters of this period evoke the relaxed routines of life away from
the front, supporting the observation that war is one part paroxysm and
nine parts idleness and boredom. For the artillery, much time is taken
up with the feeding, watering, and grooming of the horses. The chaplain organized baseball games. Card games were cruelly restricted by
the fact that there had been no payday for weeks. Many of the men had
already lost their savings and had gone into debt against the next pay-
day. I was constantly badgered for loans, and even friends who would
not gamble or buy cognac needed cash for necessities.

I also wrote to my family about the mistake of sending large parcels
of edibles, candy, and so on. The arrival of such a package in the mail-
room created a small sensation. The recipient was inevitably the prey of
a ravenous horde and was lucky if he could enjoy a small part of it.

I gave further warning about sending books in a letter to my mother
on May 26:

Books must be pocket size for me now, or none. What I want is
recreation—the classics, poetry, essays, in small form: Virgil,
Addison, "A Winter's Tale," Macauley's "Milton," "Deserted Village," "Snowbound"—one volume a week. Then I would like a good
book on New Testament criticism, up to date, say on Acts or Reve-
lation. Luther's "Table Talk."

This last item certainly reflects my college studies, and elsewhere I remark that "I am Browning through and through."

I was constantly aware that my letters had to pass under the censoring eye of one of our officers. Writing mother I said:

> No, I wasn't concealing things from you, except involuntarily. We just are not allowed to write anything. Censorship rules look liberal on paper, but when you get called up to the office in your own battery where the censoring is done, you find there is not much subject-matter. In good earnest I tell you it is a field for effort at home, to get these rules relaxed and let the men have a little of the liberty allowed newspaper correspondents.

My letters recur to the subject of the morale of the French troops. One of our hostesses said that we should not be misled by their occasional moods of revulsion and bitterness. After relaxation in a warm room, a comfortable chair, and a good cup of coffee, call on them, and their usual if protesting brio and élan will return. The French peasant stock is mercurial but has a long legacy of fiber and steel.

Near this portrait of our Gallic allies in my letter I portrayed American combatants and their different kind of resilience.

> The men are brave—for much the same lack of imagination. They have so rich a consciousness of life and pleasure that they take this very sensation as a witness against the possibility of their doing or taking harm. That's exactly what I mean to say—they feel like kings and the king can do no wrong.

No doubt one would have to put together many such soundings of either breed to get at the truth. But the historian may well take account of all such imponderables in his calculus of causes and consequences.

In the first days of June all elements of the division were rushed to the area west of Château-Thierry to parry the massive lunge of the Germans toward the Marne and Paris. Because of the restrictions of censorship this transition of our battery from the rear to the midst of the action is obscured in my letters. It is all the more surprising to find a letter written on June 4, one of the most critical days of our first salvos after a dash to our new position.

I'll have something to tell about now when we all get back. Ambulance driving may be just as risky but it doesn't approach the interest of field artillery in the "guerre de manoeuvre," and then I can't see but what I've done as high an average of cross-country sight-seeing as the ambulance sections did. . . .

If the Germans insist on forcing the issue this way, they may bore us into giving them their *coup de grace* this year instead of next. They are so tired that in making great efforts like this they are likely to slip and present us the opportunity we are looking for . . .

You can think of me as sleeping outdoors, eating out of tins, riding horseback a lot, and only harassed by those penal pistol belts and gas-masks and helmets that drag one down six inches a day. But one notices that in the strangest circumstances "time and the hour run through the longest day."

One decipherable passage in my journal corroborates with more detail the displacements of the battery in this period and my own activities.

Tue May 21

Lt Richardson and self with other billeting men left V[annault]-l[es]-D[ames] the 18th at 9 A.M.—reached V[itry]-l[e]-F[rançois], and had afternoon and evening in town. Out in box car at 9:30 P.M. with troop train of machine gun outfits (58 trains of 82nd Division). Reached Pontoise after seeing Sacré-Coeur and bombed tuberculosis hospital outside Paris. [Detrained at R——— and] by camion with billeting crews of 17th, 15th, etc. to areas for billeting out west of Paris at Lattainville.

Coincidentally, one of the hospitals was the same one to which I had evacuated the casualties arriving in Paris when I was in the Paris Section of the ambulance service was at Pontoise. During the time when we were locating accommodation for the brigade at Lattainville we slept outdoors in the warm weather. The actual billeting process for so large a personnel and horses at these stages was a complex matter. I note at one point that I handed in a roster of 1,000 men and sixty officers, for whom accommodation had been arranged for the batteries of our regiment. The troops reached us by marches and trains (in boxcars) a day or two after our arrival. These areas well behind the front, northeast and then northwest of Paris, had been largely evacuated by the civilian population, and we found rooms, granges, and stable lofts for the men, and yards and drinking troughs for the horses. The local *mairies* [town halls] were contacted for assistance.

Where families had remained, our hosts and hostesses helped us find provisions and entertained us with accounts of their experiences and those of their sons in service.

At Vannault-les-Dames I noted a piquant episode in my journal:

> Yesterday we made some leaves for the Col's mahogany mess table in the Chateau [Col. A. J. Bowley was then our new regimental commander]. The owner of the Chateau had left when the Germans advanced down past the rail-road line Bar-Paris before [Battle of the] Marne. Never came back like many of the proprietors, the many "*vides*" in the rooms and stables and granges explained by absence of men—and poor harvest.

Our stay at Lattainville at the end of May was an idyllic interlude on the brink of the frenetic drama of the days that followed. Our American division was now readied by the Supreme Command for the great German drive, and it was just a question as to where and when we would be called on to parry it.

My journal evokes the unreality of these days of waiting in the glorious landscape of the Oise when spring was at its full height. Routines went on. The men lived in the present with their customary garrulousness and byplay, seemingly oblivious of the impending ordeal into which they would be plunged. Quite apart from such forebodings it is surprising to recall that there were undercurrents of grumbling and disaffection with regard to discipline—that familiar discontent with which authority in all situations has to deal, by distraction, promises, and beguilements.

Reveille at 6. Care of horses A.M. and P.M. Detail: drill with instruments and Lt. Richardson in the field as for open warfare with
horses.

Since so many non-coms busted, much dissatisfaction among the
men. General opinion that Battery is going to the dogs. Some speak
of the good old days when Captain Brady had charge. Almost all
like Captain Reinhart, but the Lts. criss-cross things—the Davises
and Blowers, etc.

Sgt. Vencill spoke of having been dragged along 6 months with
the promise of a commission like a mule with oats under his nose.

Last night I was walking up the hill during a "vaudeville" [in
the village hall] below. Could hear the rounds of laughter and ap-
plause, witness that Carroll was at it again. I could even distinguish
the Col's voice. They said later that he had promised pay soon and
overdue tobacco rations. [He] called us "the fighting hounds of the
17th." For an hour that crowd was lost to a state of complete perdi-
tion in convulsions of uproarious laughter.

It was 8 o'clock and the scene was one to inspire thought. Around
us, in that lull, was the luxuriant foliage of the Oise, and a few
days ahead the real front! That these merry well-wishing humans
would be soon engaged in bloody battle with others in like beautiful surroundings seemed a nausea in nature much more than a mere
anachronism or contradiction.

My next entry describes a new billeting survey in the area of Beauvais, a move of the regiment which was countermanded during our absence. I recall vividly our unexpected glimpse of the Beauvais cathedral
in the distance.

Thursday May 30th

At Chambord [near Lattainville] took bike to Chaumont, and
truck there with Lt. Richardson, and billeting party. On truck from
2–5 P.M. all about Beauvais. We set up billeting headquarters in a
small town. I made arrangements for supper: eggs, milk, tomatoes,

sausages, cocoa, jam [and I note the price of each] cooked and served by an obliging matron. Got back from a little bike ride about the chateau and town to find the order countermanded. The same furious driver picks us up at 8 P.M. and we go back the same long way . . . On the way a slip of the driver lands us in a rut from which the truck is only extricated by the help of another at 2:30 A.M. Meanwhile sleep and hearing of small air-raid at Beauvais. Then jostled back to Chaumont, and back to Chambord by bike, completely exhausted (two nights without sleep) to find the Battery on the point of leaving for some other place.

With the developments of the German offensive, Pershing and the French had recognized that we were too far west to be available against the critical penetration of the Allied lines which now threatened in the Château-Thierry area. Thus we were now being rushed to that quarter.

The regimental history summarized this new phase of our activity:

Château-Thierry Defensive

The detraining points were Ormay, Dammartain and Nanteuil, the days of June 1 and 2. After a forced march of 38 kilometers complicated by the presence of many civilian refugees and retreating French soldiers, the Regiment was halted at Cocherel. On June 4 the firing batteries were moved into position in the Chateau Thierry sector. The guns, for the most part, were northwest of Chateau Thierry near Couprue and the Issange farm, department Aisne. Immediately on getting into position the batteries began firing. The first battalion (A and B batteries) claims the distinction of the first American artillery to participate in the action around Chateau Thierry which stopped the German drive toward Paris.

For a month the Regiment was actively engaged in fighting, firing every day.

The summary continues with further details about the aid we gave to our infantry in blocking the German advance on June 4 and 5, and on our later preparation and cover for them in their struggle for Belleau Wood.

My hasty jottings during the course of this historic intervention provide glimpses as seen by a participant in the ranks.

Friday, May 31, 1918

In evening Battery upstakes and out—hiking to Chaumont— loading from 5:30–9:00. In box car with 34 others. Where in creation are we going! The big new drive just started between Soissons and Rheims. In A.M. the first thing we see is cars with "Nord-Belge" on them and [we wonder if] we are going to Flanders. [I] then recognize towns (now Sat. June 1) and find to my stupefaction that we are detraining at St. Mard, about 3 kilometers from Juilly where I had been on Ambulance duty in the Paris Service [Winter 1916–17]. I had often driven to this station.

[Watering the horses.] A Frenchman reassures me that the front is still a long way off. I get a fine cheese sandwich in the café. "Saddle up!" and we are off due east on main line, Paris-Chateau Thierry. Lots of traffic. Americans welcomed with curiosity. Camions, camions, camions! Lunch in shady road after some 15 kilometers. One fellow run over by piece [gun]. Lt. Bickham calls me to go up ahead and fix the road in advance of Battery—the orders having been changed since Lt. Davis's detail [for such road work] had gone out. (They turn up at the end of the day, most of men somewhat intoxicated—pay-day three days earlier.)

We meet motorcyclist looking in vain for Headquarters which have been changed. An impression of confusion and haste farther on. Then we come to a main line of communication and see French batteries, etc., moving rapidly north toward Soissons. We go East always. Finally overtake several masses of American infantry and machine gun sections and batteries just arrived by march or truck, and press on into a town where our Regimental Headquarters are [Cocherel]. I hold horses as road-marker while the Lt. finds out where we are to billet battery and water the horses. But it is still further on, another 2 ½ kilometers, to a wood where Battery camouflages itself, and spreads its blankets after 37 kilometers march. Supper at 9:30.

For these critical days, from Sunday June 2 through Sunday June 9, I transcribe these circumstantial details of my journal (fortunately legible at this point). The division was now involved not in trench warfare but in a war of movement, and the front was changing from hour to hour. Hence the movements of our batteries were improvised and tentative, and my record reflects this confusion. Captain Reinhart was ill at this time, but he continued to command the battery. In the days that followed, after the German advance was halted and the front was stabilized, he directed the battery from a bed in a tent at our new position.

Sunday, June 2

Up at 6—feed horses—breakfast—water horses at 1 kilometer [distance]—care of materiel—going over instruments—orienting Battery position [by the coordinates on map].
I get the news for the captain (still sick). They say two Germans in American uniforms had been captured by one of the batteries. They had fired at Captain B———. A Lt. and 8 or 10 men form circle around the wood and take them and remove their American uniforms.

As I can recall it now, this episode sounds like a typical army rumor or fantasy. How did the Germans find American uniforms which fitted them and had appropriate tabs and stripes? Yet Captain Reinhart vouched for the incident. I wish I had preserved more detail on it. The infiltrators must have been selected because they knew English. They were probably spying out Allied dispositions or planning to work their way down to Paris and pick up intelligence there. The Paris métro and bulletin board everywhere carried the warning: "Les oreilles ennemis vous ecoutent!"

At this time the infantry, Marines, and machine gun sections of our division were up ahead skirmishing with the scouting parties and advance units of the enemy. In this shifting situation it was difficult to bring our batteries to position and into action.

Sound of semi-distant firing—German planes over at night. Troops of all kinds—but not in large numbers. They say there are lots of Americans up [airplanes]. Bed—ready to rise at a moment's notice.

At watering, Morgan comes galloping down and sends us all back at fast trot. Action! Orders to go up just as fast as possible. "B" and "A" move out in incredibly short time. Lt. Davis tells me to report to Lt. Blowers (Capt. Reinhart and Lt. Dixon both sick) as Battery agent to Battalion headquarters. I am to tell him that "A" Battery is ready to move out. "Follow 'B' Battery."

Out east again, along roads shielded with heavy foliage. I follow staff—hold Battalion C's horse at halts, and [that of] French interpreter.

"Present my compliments to the lieutenant commanding 'A' Battery and tell him to dismount his men during long halts. Ask him if he has received copies of the 20,000 maps." Salute and off. But I have an old plug and my spurs were packed in the thought of going for billeting. I present a ludicrous picture all the way up the column, whipping my slow charger and vainly beating his flanks with my hands. [Arrived at the Battery] I change mounts with K——— and report to B. C. S. again.

He now calls up the B. C. S. [Regimental command post] and its reconnaissance officers. We go up through a town [probably La Ferté-Milon] where there are headquarters of various American organizations, and Marines sitting and smoking in the entrance or shaving in the barns. The firing becomes very much louder. We go ahead at a fast trot. A great level country before us—full of clumps and groves of trees. One can see 3 or 4 miles and then the trees cut off the view from a country that slopes down [to the valley of the Marne to the southeast].

After a kilometer we come suddenly on a French battery firing next to the road along the edge of a wood, the small [gun] trails sunk way in deep in the ground and the pieces hidden by the foliage from above. They are firing—bark, bark—and our horses start. A little farther a battery is in position in the road itself, firing over the little bank of the adjacent fields.

We take a turn straight toward the firing—most of it ours, but I saw a shrapnel puff down there. Trot, trot, trot, dust, and brushing one another. Bang here, bang there. The Battalion Commander and the officer detailed for choosing positions go ahead. "We are now at 700 yards from the drop off of the plateau we are on. No good going over the brow! A turn into the fields and a look at the clumps of trees. It is nervous work for the officer, one can see. Detailed no doubt by Regimental headquarters.

This officer did not wish later to be blamed if a battery's location were too easily identified by enemy planes or observation balloons. In the weeks to come one or two of our batteries positioned at this time suffered direct hits, but most of them, like ours, were not directly targeted, though an occasional shell landed in our grove. The approximate position of a battery could be identified by the flashes of its guns in night firing with the help of triangulation, but this was inexact. To continue:

The officer is the English type, incisive and cold, constantly smoking, with a deformed hand and a good-sized joint in his nose. He has a kind of hotel lobby polish and no doubt knows a lot about the work. He called "B" Battery's Captain to him and discussed and assigned to him a rather spare row of poplars. Then said, "Now 'A' Battery," and poor weak Captain Reinhart [still sick at the time] and Lt. Blowers kept up with him as he trotted across the long pasture. A good deal of doubt and hesitation. Finally with a forced decision he told us to clip this fence here and take the guns into the northeast edge of that grove.

At this point the Regimental Colonel [the colorful and vociferous Bowley] comes pacing across the meadow and asks him in repeated phrases and excitement what he had done, saying, "Very well, very well," in exclamatory repetition. They then change "A" Battery to a grove closer up near a grange where it can back its guns up against the northwest/southeast edge of the grove [more convenient for firing] and fire to the northeast.

Then Battalion Headquarters are put in a grove about mid-way between, on the road, and up go wireless, and out go and in come the telephone lines to the batteries and to other Brigade Headquarters. Meanwhile we are wondering whether those Germans are coming over the edge, and if their snipers can see us, and if they will be firing on our columns visible from their captive balloons. I hold horses, guide "C" Battery Captain to our planned position, go down to tell [telephone corporal], "either stay on that damned telephone or go out and repair it." Lunch is crusts and *singe*. Then the men come back down the road with the limbers and the spare horses, to take to the echelon.

Ambulances rush up and back, going over the brow of our plateau and down to the mysterious situation below. Slightly wounded French soldiers walk back very slowly. Here is a horse that one of us has to take out and shoot because a shell fragment down there has gone through his hip (I find myself occupied). We are told of a couple of dead Marines and Frenchmen down there and a lot of wounded. In the evening the detail men come in from the observatory they have been trying to locate and tell of seeing the American infantry skirmish line advancing and falling back, the dust caused by shells, the German shells on our roads, etc. But the last thing in the world to be seen is trenches.

No shells at all up here. Occasionally a faint whistle (I can hardly write, there is so much racket—dozens of guns firing all around me) of an incoming German shell or puff of their shrapnel probably put up as a range-tester for their observers. French planes come back to and leave from a field in our proximity. Trucks begin to arrive with shells, and caisson trains go back and forth. Officers' automobiles, motorcycles, single soldiers, French batteries (rifle and howitzer) go up. The horses munch at their picket-line, and we get our three meals a day just the same. Only time flies at a furious rate and one is on edge and liable to get excited. I don't see what they want with me as "Battery Agent" now anyway. All I do is take care of my horse and be ready.

Slept in the grove with my two blankets and horse blankets and everything in place for speedy decamping in the dark. Woke up a couple of times to hear trucks unloading shells and caissons loading them for our Battery. OUR BATTERY HAD BEGUN TO FIRE ABOUT 8 P.M. (June 3), on data somehow obtained.

I capitalize here because this was an important date in our record and because there was typical interbattery rivalry then as later as to precedence in this important theatre. Our infantry was just now in the process of halting the German breakthrough.

Tuesday, June 4

It is now 11 A.M. More and more batteries in here. Wonder what the infantry is into down there. Heard the machine guns in the pauses—crackle—crackle. They are the ones that do it and suffer it all. And now most likely this offensive is stopped and we need have no great fears for the Battery with our doughboys well organized. A French *artilleur* told me yesterday of how they had lost their 4 guns (same kind) the day of the attack upon the Chemin des Dames. Here they were 8 days later going into action with new ones again.

A barrage started Tuesday night at 8:50. We were in the middle of a dozen batteries of 3″, 4.7″ and 6″ guns—French and American—all fairly outdoing themselves. One couldn't count the number per minute because the detonations were so often simultaneous. One could see the flashes from each battery—all within a radius of 700 or 800 yards. It kept up for 45 minutes and then resumed for a half an hour later. There was harrassing fire all night too. Once in a long while a lone *arrivé* would whistle and burst some way off. It was like a man with a cannon opposing a man with a pop gun. The Germans rely on infantry in this kind of warfare.

Rumors of different kinds but none of them trustworthy.

"The 75's were firing on their own troops who had to 'f——— le camp.'"
"There were only 30 meters between the Boche and us and the men only had little 3-foot ditches for protection."
"Our troops at St. Mihiel, etc., have gotten into Germany and are approaching Metz."
"The French took 25,000 prisoners east of Château Thierry by leaving a bridge standing until the Germans had passed then destroying it by charges already laid and closing in."

None of these rumors have the least foundation probably. What seems established is that the Germans are no longer advancing—

that they have practically no artillery—that their superiority in numbers is very great—that there are Moroccans and Senegalese units fighting and 3 American divisions here (though not referred to in reports). We seem to be at the very southwest corner of the big salient the enemy has opened up. A Frenchman said that even at the first success the morale of the German troops was poor: They realized they would be stopped here as in their big push at Amiens and Kemmel.

B——— said our officers at Hdq. were very much discouraged yesterday because the French were even still giving a little ground while backed by all the artillery they would ultimately have, while the Germans had hardly any of theirs yet.

In that deafening barrage last night there was a convoy of trucks just beside my shelter roaring their engines for starting off and a little yellow dog by my blankets, barking frantically, but the dog was the worst of all. It's the impudence, the Personality in sound that makes it rasping.

It was during these days of June that the American Marines and regulars, encouraged by the increasingly massive support of our batteries, brought the German advance to a halt. Their platoons, advancing under fire "through the wheat" (the title of a book written in 1923 by Thomas Boyd) and dodging through the trees and thickets, repelled the enemy capturing and overrunning their machine gun nests. From this point on the battle, the war itself had a different character. As Victor Hugo writes in his *Châtiments*, at the Battle of Waterloo when delayed reinforcements came over the horizon and were seen, to the dismay of Napoleon, not to be those of Ney but of Blucher come to join Wellington:

Le conflit changea de face, le combat changea d'âme.

At this point I introduce an account of this juncture in the Great War written by Samuel T. Williamson in 1938.

Ever since [Ludendorff's drive in March, threatening the Channel ports] the Germans had been on the offensive and close to winning the war. Late in May they scooped out a deep salient between

Rheims and Soissons as far as the Marne and lunged toward Paris. By this time allied reserves were at the bottom of the barrel. Parisians were scampering out of the city, and the government prepared to send its papers to Bordeaux—what it actually did when the field-gray swarms reached the Marne four years before.

Two days before Memorial Day, the First Division took Cantigny, and this first relatively large-scale action by the Americans was sufficient proof to Marshal Foch that the young men from across the Atlantic qualified as shock troops. Thus encouraged, he placed another American division, the Second, across the German path to Paris. It may be too much to say that one division by itself saved Paris. But the stand of the division's infantry brigade across the Metz-Paris road and the marine brigade's desperate venture in Belleau Wood, resulting not only in stopping the enemy but in throwing him back, came at one of the great crises of the war; and it galvanized the low-spirited French defense. In that sense marines and regulars did save Paris.[5]

As imaginative overtone to my reminiscences I have occasionally cited poems from my 1923 collection, *Battle-Retrospect* (Yale Series of Younger Poets), written shortly after the war but suffused with the immediate experience. As transcriptions in a higher octave of my original sense of the import of events, and despite all their hyperbole and literary shortcomings, they reflect the sensibility of a young combatant involved in these momentous transactions.

Belleau, June 1, 1918

In that fair month that saw the final stand,
When France was splintered and convulsed with throes,
As, in the armies of the black-helmed foes,
Chaos thrust forth his fingers o'er the land,
And, as when seas encroach upon a strand,
Moved, an immeasurable flood of Night,
Across the spring, while men and beasts in flight
Avoided the dark terror close at hand;
We, bearing in us the decree of God,

The *ne plus ultra* to the mindless urge
Of the unordered universe, the surge
Of Chaos, to that shelving border trod,
Halted and turned the tide, and saw emerge
Again the flowering valleys from the flood.

No doubt any such theological reading of our action would have been
far from the thoughts of those engaged. Yet it is remarkable how generally the soldiery of all wars are persuaded that higher powers, if only
fate or some vague idea of nemesis, overrule the fortunes of battle.

A couple of messages to Captain R[einhart]. [I am now evidently
not at the Battery, but back at the echelon.] At dusk showed way
up past the Grange where Marine Hdqs are—down thru fields to
"A" Battery. Five trucks unloaded there. The boys wearing their gas
suits for practice. Said they fired over 100 rounds per gun preceding
night. German division being relieved. Saw a nearby saucisse [bal-
loon] brought down by a squad of 7 Boche [planes]. One dived 45° a
long way—the balloon[ist] asleep—pop, pop, and up he glides—
flame [while observer parachutes]. All French machine guns open
up . . . in rage.

The German artillery apparently arrived. A couple of duds in
our back lot. A 17th corporal carried down stretcher case in ambulance.—Today, Thur. 6th, about 18 German prisoners conducted
down the road. Marines say they took 400 and 4 kilometers this
A.M. A paper (yesterday) tells of us Americans N. W. of Château
Th[ierry] and on the Marne. Clemenceau's struggle with the Socialists in Chamber. People in the *arrière* more worked up than those at
the front . . .

There seem to have been about 1000 prisoners taken. A conversation between two Marines:
"What did you want to take them prisoners for? Why didn't you
shoot the d——s?"
"That's the way I felt about it," said the other. "But if you could
seen them on their knees praying with tears in their eyes, saying
'Kamerad, Kamerad,' you wouldn't have the heart."

I moved down yesterday (Thur. 6th) to the Battery [from the eche-lon], Cpl. Clayton replacing me as Battery Agent. The night shift cannoneers came over about 7 with the grub from the echelon. A half a dozen big German shells fell all around us about 8 P.M., making us feel pretty tickled without any dugouts or anything. This morning Wharton is digging himself a trench.

Last night and this A.M. I am reading Jeanne d'Arc before send-ing it to Alfred Chochod. [See Part I on the Paris Section and ambulance driving.] A great reproach and restorative . . . Some-times one cannot but think that there is a direct intervention in the coming to hand of a book or even a page.

The next few pages of my day-to-day jotting record the days in which our batteries supported the assault of our Marines and infantry on Bel-leau Wood and its environs. This was one of the most decisive actions of the American forces in the war, one in which they not only halted the German drive on Paris but also began the counterincursions on the enemy lines which led through summer and fall to the success of the Allies on the entire front. During these critical engagements of our divi-sion in June my assignment included regulation of our battery's fire with our officers from advanced observation posts.

Friday 7th—Yesterday went to the O.P. [observation post] on horseback with Lt. Davis and Cpl. Glorvigen. Rode a couple of kilo-meters along a road from which we could see the disputed country for miles through the intervals between the clumps of trees. Marines in woods—food camouflaged—sleeping in little dug-out places big enough for one. [We go] up in a tree with glasses, telephone. Our targeting on a farmhouse.

A Marine (U. of Minn.) tells about classmates killed with half the battalion the night before. Some platoons still out there in those woods without communication, may be prisoners—don't know where they are.

More German shells in afternoon and during a barrage at night. Battery now almost vacated. Captain, Lt. Dixon, Lt. Davis, Lt.

Billingsly, Lt. Blowers, the 4 dayshift gun crews, Vencill and 3 telephone men—no horses—rest at echelon . . .

Sat. night, 8th

Today we were going to O.P. but Lt Davis busy with big problem for tonight—a two-hour 40 minute problem—all our six batteries and a lot of others. First preparation—then a couple hours more of rolling barrage and harrassing fire. I saw the tracing paper with the assignment of times and targets laid over the Captain's map. Bois de B[elleau], a couple kilometers objective [probably underestimated here]. The Battery firing regularly every day—crossroads, woods, buildings, towns.

Thursday, June 13

Every A.M. for the last four or five days there has been heavy barraging at dawn, following steady firing all night. We are directly opposite the Bois de Belleau which I think taken yesterday by the Marines. Went up to the tree-post yesterday horseback with Lt. Davis, Partelow and Lieber. Shell holes all way up. The tree I observed from last time blown down by a shell. [A]bout to register on our old farmhouse when a Marine said it now belongs to the Americans!—

Went to bed Wednesday night with this terrible itch and didn't sleep till 4:45. The barrage and sound of fighting about 3:30–4:15 was fascinating. Firing from all these Batteries—German shrapnel and H.E. [high explosive] arriving around—the barrages in the distance on sectors to our left and right. The clicks of the shells shoved home and closing breech blocks—"Ready," "Fire" and we are shaken on our blankets. The intervals of rounds filled with that awesome machine gun fire. The exchanges slowed down and I went to sleep finally.

The Marines our whole Second Division making a record for self. "Road to Paris!"

Battery shelled with German 150's. Vencill and I in a 3 foot trench. The roar and the proximity [of these shells] something ferocious. Gas!—eyes smart—masks for 15 minutes. Battery has fired once under direct fire.

Yesterday "B" Battery shelled with 240's. Tremendous holes, absolutely no harm! Aeroplane observation . . . The Marines tell us how applauded our barrages are.

The Seventeenth Regimental History summarizes the later days of our Batteries' activity in the Château-Thierry sector, our brief period in the rear, and our subsequent involvement in the decisive American action near Soissons in the Villers-Cotterets attack of July 18 and following.

For a month the Regiment was actively engaged in fighting, firing every day . . . to make preparation for the attacks of our own infantry; . . . After stopping the Germans on June 4 and 5 the Americans took the offensive. This feat of the Second Division marks the turning point of the fighting in 1918. Up to this point the Germans had done all the driving. After the Allies began their series of successful attacks, they regained practically all they had lost in the spring.

The 17th Field Artillery participated in the successful assaults on the Bois de Belleau, Bouresches, Vaux and Hill 204. Vaux in particular, on July 1, was completely demolished by the terrific fire of the 155's . . . Frequently the German artillery opened fire on the battery positions, but their fire was not so accurate nor destructive . . .

Soissons:

After a month of continuous fighting the Regiment was relieved on July 7 and 8 by the 103rd F. A. of the 26th ["Yankee"] Division . . . and went back into reserve northeast of La Ferté-sous-Jouarre. On July 11 and 12, however, the batteries were moved to more advanced positions.

The evening of Sunday, July 14, the Regiment received orders to march immediately to the wood near Betz. The march was begun a short time after midnight. There was no moon but the sky was clear and the stars gave sufficient light for traveling. Our destination was reached about noon of the 15th. Shortly after arrival the Commanding Officer received orders to return to the area just vacated, but later in the afternoon the order was changed to proceed to a point in the Forêt de Villers-Cotterets near Haremont. Shortly after 8 P.M. the Regiment started again. It hiked throughout the night and the next morning, reaching its position early in the afternoon of the 16th.

This summary continues in greater detail through the strenuous days of Mangin's attack on the German salient and the relief of our division on July 25, leading to its entrainment to the Toul area for rest and reconstitution on the banks of the Moselle.

My own assignments shifted in this period; from being on the instrument detail (observation post adventures, and so on) I became ammunition corporal in the later weeks of June, and then went back to billeting duties when the battery was relieved and in the rear.

The ammunition assignment was by far the most difficult, and this was the most exhausting experience of my service overseas, especially because I was not fitted for it. The shells, powder bags, and fuses were unloaded from trucks at night in our grove (at night to avoid observation of our battery position). My role was that of foreman over a dozen often weary men as they piled the ninety-pound shells in tiers in the dark in shallow trenches, so that the uppermost layer would be below the surface of the ground (like our "beds") for greater security against flying shrapnel or shell fragments. So also with the powder bags and fuses. To police this operation in the small hours of the night was hard enough, but in addition I had to keep exact account of the ammunition at any given time which varied with the number of items unloaded. On one occasion Captain Reinhart called me in for a discrepancy in my figures which was vital to our battery's "mission" at the time but which it was almost impossible to avoid.

Because I was now always with the advanced combat section and not back at the echelon (wagon train), one disagreeable assignment I rarely had was the stable detail with its never ceasing exasperations with the care of the horses, especially leading them to crowded or distant watering troughs. With my own single mount I shared, however, the fatigues indicated in the letters below when after an unsettled period in the rear we were involved in all-night forced marches leading to the Soissons offensive. One learned to doze in the saddle at halts, but the excitement of the following days of the great attack and advance covered over a persisting tiredness which was only relieved when many days later the division was rusticated far to the east by the Moselle.

The special elation of the celebration of Independence Day in Paris, relayed by my *marraine de guerre*, Blanche Stanley, was prompted by the repulse of the German threat to the city and this outcome of the Second Battle of the Marne. Just a year before we were at Lafayette's grave when, shortly after reaching France, Pershing there acclaimed our American arrival on the scene and honored the bonds of Franco-American comradeship in arms. I wrote to my family:

July 12

Miss Stanley writes of the Paris "Fourth" as being a day which will probably be considered as epoch-making as that of Magna Carta. More so than the Day of Victory because the suffering is still going on and the rejoicing partakes of faith more than of relief.

What a series of expectations, changes and surprises for us lately! And now we are more or less "en repos," although at this time nobody is allowed to sleep with both eyes closed, or far from the lines. All war stories tell of the deliciousness of the first "rest" in camp. My! If I could only tell you my blessed relief and happiness when I inventoried and turned over to the relieving battery all our ammunition. I felt as though I had dropped the whole actual weight of steel and powder off my shoulders. . . . There we got our single mounts and rode delirious through the rain and starlight to a rear position. A couple hours of sleep and breakfast. Then fixing bunks up in the green-wood, and sleep, sleep, sleep! I luxuriated in it for 48 hours and wondered at the energy some of the men seemed to show, washing their clothes, making "off-the-ground" bunks, shooting crap, writing letters, etc. I just turned over on the other side and went to sleep again until somebody tickled my bones and said "Come and get it" (chow). The woods are so green and the sound of firing so removed and Turnbow's old melodeon is so new-inspired! You see one becomes quite irrelevant. Anyway, it's great! Only we worry a little that the great work of our famous division may not be upheld by our replacers. They were National Guard men, noticeably well-washed and good-looking; but we had to laugh at the deliberateness in between rounds. Of course they didn't want to get the gun hot! But then! At any rate we violated all French rules about speed and maximum number of rounds, and old "Woodrow Wilson" and "Betsy Ross" [the nicknames of our howitzers] are still speaking with great force and precision.

Today I reverted to my old ambulance job of purchasing agent for the table (the officers' mess in this case). Got a horse and saddle bags and trotted about the countryside looking for eggs, jam, tea, canned goods, etc. By dint of return trips and waiting in French line, which is no line at all (just a push where assertiveness wins) I got the last pound of butter, nearly fainting from the immediacy of disaster; and everything else except eggs. That requires a peculiar "scent"; one must have an intuition like the hazel stick that locates water or treasure—to find eggs in the *zone des armées*. On the side, I supplement or rather substitute for my own rations, so as to avoid meat and coffee. I notice a recurrent feverishness, though slight, and a nervousness and restlessness that recur likewise periodically, daily—and it is fierce sometimes. I attribute it to body lice which have bothered all of us for the last three or four weeks. Now we have just been issued light underclothes and I'm going to carry cleanliness to the point of absurdity while we have the chance. The German drive will probably renew its youth one of these days and spoil our fun.

In [Washington] Irving I came across this which I recall strikingly: "His self respect is kept alive by finding that though all abroad is darkness and humiliation, yet there is still a little world of love at home, of which he is a monarch." Curious opiate to mediocrity! Therefore nothing but confidence, and the greater love to you all.

My next letter, July 14, is to Thornton. The contents indicate that he was then in Washington, D.C. Thanks to Gilbert Harrison's extensively researched biography (*The Enthusiast*), I am reminded that after the close of his junior year at Yale and in lieu of more active enlistment (from which he was dissuaded by those who knew his aptitudes and by the fact of his poor vision, he had found a position with the War Industries Board as clerk and office boy. Thornton, however, had "fits of militancy" which led to his induction in the Coast Guard Artillery Corps at Newport, R.I. in September where he served as orderly and typist until the Armistice and for three months after until he was released to return to Yale.

I was astonished at the date of the letter, for on July 14 my battery was about to be catapulted (the 15th) into two sleepless nights of forced march to the Villers-Cotterets staging area. Although the letter does not touch on such actualities and is slanted more to introspection, it shares with Thornton the quandary of the dreamer and the aspiring artist in the nets of public and military hierarchy. One is reminded of the refrain of the popular song of the time: "I didn't raise my boy to be a soldier." Thornton, indeed, belonged to the order of the hummingbird and the chameleon and could not well be martialed into such a regimented system.*

Sunday, July 14

Dear Thornton—

I'm answering your letter of April 3. Our correspondences have a tone of sweet condolence about them as though we were both in the house of bondage. I try to subdue the attitude that this is but a task "passagère"—and to learn to like the work, but it is in vain. There seems to be a fundamental incompatibility of my temperament and the idea of military organization. One can't orient himself in an hierarchy of authority without giving a sad farewell to many gentle ways and actions. If I do this can I resurrect them afterwards? But it seems necessary that a corporal learn to be harsh. So behold me selling my birthright to keep up the traditions of the Regular Army.

*Thornton Wilder volunteered for service in the Second World War, serving with Air Force intelligence in North Africa and Europe and ending the war as a colonel. Paul Horgan recalls asking him why he had not chosen a softer, more literary billet. The reply: "Never. I shall not write for my country!"

My thought of an army discipline is probably too much like the Bolchevikis' [sic]—"democratization of the army"—everybody working together with a will, like a family on the frontier. The faults with this are (1) the planners or leaders tire themselves so much that their leadership is less trustworthy (2) it doesn't take into account the shirkers, who have to be dealt with like bad children.—Anyway, I've been reprimanded lately for not being enough of a soldier—not for failure to obey all orders, certainly—but for insufficient display of authority.—I think I can solve the matter by diluting the strictness with fairness and—on the outside of "duty"—being more of a good fellow. Anyway you see my problems.—The other day a fellow directed towards me a filthy suggestion—entirely in fun—one passed any number of times among the other men. I "called" him—i.e.—protested strongly. He got mad, but is now amicable. It probably did him good, and I have already a more respectful position. Some of them call me John the Baptist! I may have to slap somebody's face one of these days if these remarks are repeated (I don't mean calling me Jn the Baptist which I laugh at) and thus get myself into a scrap around the corner—but it is absolutely necessary if I am to earn any respect. After that things will go a lot easier. The fellows certainly learn some nasty habits of speech and a stand from somebody in true army fashion is the only way out.

My confidence about your writing is as great or greater than yours. You must be allowed that drill and exercise in it which success in any line demands. At the same time I believe thoroughly now in the background of experience—even apparently irrelevant and irksome experience. This is the condition of that growth in conception and conceits and fancies and thoughts and inventions and spontaneities. . . .

Your very affectionate brother
Amos

111

✳

July
1918

Thornton's attention to the war at that time is attested by a fabulous short script published in the Yale literary magazine in 1918. It seems the editors had arranged some sort of symposium under the theme "In Praise of Guynemer." George Guynemer was a French aviator, the ace of aces, who in solitary combat had attained a semi-mythical prestige in downing one after the other of the German notorious rulers of the skies, with seeming immunity to peril. Thornton's tribute to his undying fame reads as follows:

> There is a kind of doctrine abroad in France that tribute due the dead, that is to the humble, unknown dead of the trenches, may be paid to Guynemer, because in the great days of the first two years they looked up from their trenches to his airplane, and murmuring "Guynemer," gazed on their hope. The farmer's son has no tablet in the Pantheon, save that to Guynemer, nor the peddlar's son, and so on.
>
> This veneration will grow. His place is beside the heroes he mused upon. And in distant ages when scholars shall say patronizingly of references to this war: "No doubt there was a struggle of some kind"; when our records, having passed under the contempt of a rising race, shall be neglected and lost; and the nationality of Shakespeare will be held in dispute, and of the remaining plays it will be denied that Hamlet and Twelfth Night are from the same hand; and Virgil shall become the name of a mood and Dante of a shaking dream; and our language shall be mixed with the Chinese as oil and water are mixed; and an aerial kingdom shall hang suspended over the South Sea islands; and scholars be poking about for Rheims, as now they do for the Skaian Gate;—in after time Guynemer shall rise, like Hector undoubtable from a mythic war. Georges Guynemer descends History, like a stream down the face of a mountain, making the whole green, and from time to time reappearing in springs and waterfalls.

This exercise in virtuosity and imaginative excursions, when a junior in college, anticipates the iridescence of his first novel, *The Cabala*, which he began to write two years later in Rome and which was published in 1926.

Here was one kind of heroism which was immune to the general deflation of heroics and valor which became so widespread with the accumulating costs of the war. Does it not testify that human nature will always have a residual veneration despite all cynicism for the fortitude of all those well-known or unknown who "dare the unpastured dragon in his den"?

[To my sister Charlotte]

I suppose all your friends' brothers are officers. I'll endeavour to satisfy your family pride outside the army some day. I rode back to the horse camp last night leading a horse and escorting an officer. It was a beautiful scene. The valley of one of the great rivers; one could see miles and there was color in the clouds. First time I have forgotten the war for a long time. I thought if only one were seeing this from the point of view of an innocent bicycle trip with a brother or sister or friends. Maybe in that case it wouldn't look so good though. There are subjective components in all beauty, I guess. Duty isn't so bad a one.

July 22

I am busy all day and a good part of the night. We are in the big affair, rushed into it on time by a mere few moments to spare, relieved after much praise and return to the battle by our own insistence. Everybody is tired but hopeful, almost jubilant as the reports come in. I am at the old ammunition job, and they just put another man in to take it at night in time, or I would have gone under, health and reputation to boot; but last night I was relieved at 7 p.m., and had a most glorious sleep. The reason I dislike taking time even to write this is that I am a good deal of a bonehead, it seems, in these things; and especially I can't add or think when tired out. But I guess it'll work out O.K. It's the riding that tires me, and then one's clothes, washing, shaving, appearance, go all to pieces in a time like this. I admire the officers with a new admiration and am surprised that I ever thought myself anywhere near capable of putting forth the same unrelenting energy without arriving finally at disheartenment or loss of composure. I don't see how they do it. No mail, not much comes through these jammed roads but the necessaries. We have an "A" battery "junior" in the addition to our family

of a German gun, duly turned around and all ready with its own
ammunition.

I suppose there is a mere chance that this last couple weeks'
work will start the German avalanche on its way, and October 1
might well see us through.

I'm at my old job of billeting again. Right now I'm on a sunny
crossroad waiting for one of the batteries to come along so I can
show them where to water their horses, where to stretch their picket
lines; where to pitch their tents, where to put their materiel, and
where the officers sleep in the village. Each house, in the army
zone, has on it "—Officers"; "—Men"; "—Horses." We Billeters
go ahead of the organizations when they are on the move and prepare the way, that is to say, we claim the cream of the village in
the way of edibles—eggs, butter, milk, roast beef. And how good
they are after the "front," and its series of snatched meals—mostly
"monkey meat."

We have had a very strenuous time. We have been in the middle
of the biggest things going on in June and July, and have been right
with the American infantry that has done the most, that is Chateau
Thierry, and later, the Villers-Cotterets advance. We were to have
been relieved a couple times, but remained at our own request until
the critical period was over and until our fatigue really endangered
the contribution we could make. Meanwhile we have had citations
and won all kinds of congratulations. Our regiment has about the
best reputation for artillery in the American Army.

I can't tell much of it. I can write letters to you in my notebook for my return. We fired one morning and the same day went
into position in territory which in the morning was a long way inside the German lines. Talk about souvenirs—actual and visual!
One day we occupied five different positions, up and back, nearly
having a brush with the German infantry once. You can judge what
a time it was for keeping up the ammunition end. There was plenty
of German ammunition around, but it was a job to get at our own
ammunition when we were moving around so fast. I got so tired that

I finally didn't care and they saw they'd have to give me some help. At the end we got in a lot of projectiles, etc., and slid the whole bunch of them "over" between 3 and 8 a.m., and that evening were relieved. And the next day the paper tells about the victory the barrage made possible and our French hosts congratulate us. We were firing a lot of German ammunition out of a captured German gun, too, with a crew made up of all the extra men around—one mule skinner [driver], one telephone corporal, one machine gunner, one water carter (Mike, the joke of the battery). We were just in an open field, hardly any camouflage; half the battery firing, and two-thirds of it asleep (an overlapping, you see). No extra energy for cleaning up, or anything except the essentials, getting ammunition, firing and keeping the guns clean. For the rest, let 'er slide! We had pretty good food all the time. Also it rained quite a little.

Strange when one is tired, it not only affects one's physical force, but one's powers of addition, memory, the presence and bearing of the person, his greeting and authority, but most strangely, one's conscience, one's ethical standard is blurred and one becomes curiously lax. The artillery pays in fatigue and depletion what the infantry pays in wounds and suffering. Worst of all, one becomes too worn down to pray. Well, only like a tired child, without raising the eyes. I still feel this way and am glad others are praying for me.

August 4 (near Nancy)

We are behind the lines some 15 or 20 miles in an entirely new and quiet sector. We were in the very thick of it from June 1 to very recently. Except for a few repairs to be made and a little rest to be had, we are in good shape and ready for more. Especially the heavier branch of field artillery—such as ours—seems fairly well protected from heavy disaster. But now the material goes to the mobile repair shop, the horses to graze, the men on short passes and light duty . . .

The most interesting day we had was the following: at 7 p.m. we started our material on the march from the rear to the gun locations already selected. There was to be an extensive attack the following morning at 4:30, at least the artillery was to begin at that time and

the infantry very shortly after. All we knew of this though could only
be gathered from the fearful amount of forward traffic on the roads.
These preparations were taking place in a thickly-wooded region
and the weather for a couple of days had been favorable to concealment of the unusual activity. The roads were jammed with caissons,
supply wagons, staff cars, ammunition trucks, machine gun trains
and literally hundreds (I saw them) of tanks. It seemed as though
the great mass of troops destined for the attack were poured into the
sector that last night. There was a swarming, a confusion, a density, an activity that was rather awesome to watch. And all taking a
course finally in those middle hours of the last night for the front.
Think of the organization! At any rate, our battery had its position
arranged for; the targets assigned; ranges and deflections and varia-
tions all down on paper. It seemed all arranged, except that the
guns were not in position. Starting at 8 p.m. the evening before,
guns, caissons, wagons, with more ammunition, one officer's wagon,
a wagon for the men's packs, the cannoneers on foot—it seemed
there would be plenty of time. But it turned out that there was such
a congestion of roads that only a great effort made it possible for "A"
Battery to have its guns laid in time. They were ready just in the
nick of time; two of the four with enough ammunition to start. There
had been one long enforced halt at an impossible narrow bridge
and steep hill where teams had to be transferred and the men had
to get on the wheels, where there were caissons coming back and
room hardly for one column where Frenchmen and Americans became furious at each other. There was a machine gun outfit blocked
behind us at the time they were supposed to go over the top. I was
back with the wagons when suddenly the barrage started all around
us. Whatever preparations might be incomplete, the sudden tremendous fire began inexorably at the set time—the dozens and
dozens of batteries (moved that night into open field and along the
woods and roads), opened up at their highest rate per minute.
The quiet sector was transformed in a moment into pandemonium.
The air filled with squadrons of planes—the enemy's arriving
quickly on the scene to bomb the batteries whose [flashes] still

came out bright in the half-dawn, and which were clearly revealed
an hour later because of the inattention to cover. No order about the
batteries. Shells unloaded at the guns and fired off with any kind
of fuse, the men carrying up ammunition to the crew, and the officers on the telephone and at the firing chart. When we came up with
the rest of the wagons finally we had to dash down a road ¼ mile
long, which was lined with French and American batteries that were
firing like machine guns right across the road we were going down.
They would stop an instant to let us pass, waving us on and cheering and laughing, and "letting 'em go" almost before we had gotten
out of the way.

There seemed to be all kinds of enthusiasm. This was soon
heightened by the news that the attack had come up to all expectation, the infantry was advancing by the kilometer, a whole bunch
of German guns already captured; we would probably have to move
up soon. Indeed, after an hour's firing, we stopped. The kitchen
was there and everybody hungry and in high spirits. In the afternoon we got orders to go up, loaded on the rest of our ammunition
and took the road right through the trenches into what was Boche
land. By this time, they had retreated six or eight kilometers and
were still going. The signs along the road of the recent fighting were
very few. One dead German is all I saw. There were some wounded.
It seems to have been a walk-away. But the action going on all the
time was the most interesting: the taking up of new positions, the
sight of different troops, cavalry, tanks, armored motor cars, aeroplanes, Scotch, British, Africans, Americans. Oh! It was a pageant
and nobody thinking what they looked like. No time for noticing the
signs of German occupation with German street signs on our paths,
the names on their dugouts (One was "Walderuhe.") The half-drunk
beer bottles on their tables; the piles of German ammunition, etc.
Neither had one time to collect impressions, memories of the men,
scenes on the road, etc. One walked blindfold (by feverish preoccupation) through a scene that painters will paint and historians
describe for centuries. The best things never come to us face to
face, but get by us in a disguise or in some deceptive way before we

can know it and appreciate it. One felt it though in a headlong sort of way. Next day we moved up again.

My entries at this time are full of gaps during this phase of shifting orders, forced marches, and then the last rush through the deep forest to the opening of the attack at 4:35 A.M. on July 18. General Mangin was successful in surprising the forces of the crown prince by this last-minute mobilization of our troops—including our American First and Second Divisions and French and Moroccan divisions—in the forest of Villers-Cotterets, the concealment aided by occasional rain. He thus struck eastward at the rear of the German salient when they were looking for our Allied counter-offensive at their advance penetration to the south.

Villers-Cotterets Woods

July 20, 2 P.M. [Date of entry]

July 7th, finally relieved by a Battery of the 26th [the well known "Yankee Division"] after thinking that our relief had been postponed by German offensive preparations opposite. The last two days we worked day and night digging pits for the guns with the idea of staying the Germans' last great push to last gun and man. When this work done the position handed over to new crews to the disgust of our Battery.

Back at midnight to [our] first echelon, then by horse to woods at Cocherel. On the 8th into reserve position (our caissons full) in old halt-camp up road 1 kilometer. Three days later into new reserve position . . . I spent each day on horseback buying extras for officers' mess . . . The whole countryside strewn with lines of defense before expected powerful German offensive. Thus our reserve Battery too.

At midnight 14th, flashes to the East, later recognized to be the great [German] "Offensive de la Paix," the other side of Chateau Thierry, just beginning its artillery preparation.

Our whole Division on the road—Cocherel to Luzy-sur-Ourcq, then north, midnight to 11 A.M., a fatiguing march to a camp in woods. Breakfast and watering horses the 15th at rest camp where also 4th Division troops. Lunch at 3 P.M. after feeding horses, etc.

Orders to pull out at 7 P.M. Left 9 P.M. The 16th hiked, hiked, hiked all night and all day, very slowly account of traffic and fatigue. Stopped at 11 A.M. for breakfast and lunch on a hill way west of Villers-Cotterets Woods for which we were heading. Then on again till 3 P.M. when we passed into the Villers-Cotterets woods from the plain (where German balloons could see us easily). [Came] to a town where I bought some paté and cheese (Crème de Gruyère) for officers and self, with something also for orderlies.

Rejoined column and detail. On, on—very tired out, horses and men, till we began to pass camps of the 15th and 12th [Regiments—our Division] in the middle of Woods . . .

The traffic in these main thoroughfares is something marvelous. Signals attack. French [including Moroccans] and Americans. Then what seemed a thousand tanks at least rolled by, the French drivers looking through their opened doors and in shirt sleeves. Traffic blocked at times for 10 or 15 minutes at a time. Infantry—artillery columns—caisson trains—ambulances—staff cars—machine gun carts (one horse)—supply wagons and rolling kitchens—dispatch-riders—Military Police—cyclists—trucks, trucks, trucks.

Bivouacked finally. Water, feed horses. So ended 16th July. Then one night's sleep after 2 nights and 1 day no sleep. All [next] day, 17th working. I took "A" and "B" Battery wagons to ammunition dumps for loading.

That night was the great one. Rumors that the attack was to begin next A.M. at 4. No one could believe it, for troops, tanks, etc. so far behind lines. But that night at 8 P.M. (17th) the movement ahead began. On both sides of the road through immense woods, under clouds that for several days had favored surprise, went the infantry (American 2nd division Marines and [49th?] and 23rd) and French. Between our artillery columns, with trucks and French trying to break [through] it, and officers riding back and forth to watch continuity. Torn trees, great shell holes to avoid—banks crumbling at side of road—great trucks stuck or thrown out of the way on their sides to open road—brakes refusing to work and [the] movement upset, horses unable to hold on hill and great weighted vehicles re-descending and threatening to crush those behind. German aeroplanes dropping intense slow-burning flares that lighted great area and dropping bombs. Congestion of the road and a standstill for 5 hours with officers frantic. French and American in violent opposition and discussion. The shelled bridge over the stinking pond with steep and narrow impossible ascent beyond.

4 A.M. coming [nearer], and those guns and shells had to be there [ready] to fire. The French machine gun corps! behind us at 4 and supposed to go over the top at that time a mile ahead! Would it all be a failure—would they postpone everything for another day or 2 days till all could be ready? No, too many advantages lost.

Suddenly at 4:35 the most violent bombardment imaginable broke out around us—still stuck back there in that ascending valley helpless—but the guns and some rounds had gotten up to our position. They were laid in the dark with Sgt. Vencill's aid with lights. And "A" Battery opened up on its area at 4:33 just 3 minutes late, but the first Battery in the 17th [to fire]—last battery to get into position. 150 rounds were fired. Meanwhile we in the rear with our ammunition and supplies got over that hill by hitching extra teams—getting French aid on wheels—clearing the road amid imprecations from the French by pure arbitrariness—and came galloping down a road to the front, behind which was a battery every 50 or 100 feet firing right across the road at an elevation to take in our horses and wagons. The French and Americans warned us to speed by so as not to interfere too much with their barrage—waited for us to get by and then fired almost into us.—On we galloped till we came to our own smoking guns—the active and resting crews (exhausted with 4 or 5 hours pushing up the guns on that bad road).

This the A.M. of the 18th soon good news came in. The doughboys have carried everything before them. We'll probably have to move out and up closer. 105 German guns captured—advanced several kilometres—prisoners coming in in droves. Squadrons of aeroplanes overhead fighting, bombing, observing.

This close-up account of the night and morning of the Soissons attack, like a telescope reversed, is very different from that of a military histo-

rian. The barrage at 4:35 extended for 120 miles east, to the Argonne, so that the enemy would not know at what point an attack would be pressed. A new commander of the Second Division, General James G. Harbord, had just been appointed during the rush to the new front and he did not know for some time where the division was nor what orders it had received. Harbord, as major, had commanded the Marines in the Belleau area and now as major general was placed in charge of the whole division on the eve of a new battle when it was moving under changing orders to a concealed front which he had not himself reconnoitered. This kind of confusion highlights the imperative secrecy of the attack and helps to explain the difficulties of its theatre and timing during those last hours preceding it.

To my eyewitness record, this mole's-eye notation out of the density of the historic action as registered by one participant, I add a version of that night and morning conveying a higher perception of its import, an essential dimension of any adequate rehearsal of the event. Several years later I wrote my still-vivid memory of it in a poem entitled "Armageddon: Forêt de Villers-Cotterets, July 18, 1918" (published in my *Arachne: Poems* in 1928). I cite here only the opening verses, which were preceded by this note:

> The crux and turning-point of the World War is usually assigned to the dawn of July 18, 1918. At that time, after a feverish mobilization in the great woods near Soissons of Highlander, Moroccan, and other units, including the first and second American divisions, General Mangin, under Marshall Foch's orders, attacked eastward, threatening the German Marne salient. The desperate rush to the front in the great beech forests during that rainy night and the attack at 4:35 remain one of the outstanding epic actions of the war. The overtones of the event and its portentous significance were obscurely felt by those who took part in it.

> Was it a dream that all one summer night
> We toiled obscurely through a mighty wood
> Teeming with desperate armies; toiled to smite
> At dawn upon the unsuspecting height

Above, the Powers of Darkness where they stood?
Was it a dream? Our hosts poured like a flood

In ceaseless cataract of shadowy forms
Along the dark torrential avenues.
Within, the host unseen, unseeing, swarms;
Without, the blind foe's nervous shell-fire storms,
And groping plane its flares, suspicious, strews
Above the cross-roads where the columns fuse.

Dwarfed in the enormous beeches and submerged
In double night we labored up the aisles
As in an underworld; our convoys surged
Like streams in flood, and now our torrents merged
With other torrents from the blind defiles
As hurrying units joined our crowded files.

The hoarse confusion of that precipitate march,
The night-long roar that hung about that train,
Lost itself in the branches that o'erarch
Those passages, and to the heaven's far porch
No whisper rose, but all that agonized strain
Of myriads clamored to the skies in vain.

Beneath a load of palpable dark we bowed.
Smothered in hours with time itself we strove.
The wilderness stood o'er us like a cloud
Opaque to bar bright futures disallowed,
Denying dawn, as though the vindictive grove
Eternal night around our legions wove.

Was it a dream, that rush through night to day?
Far in the depths of night we labored on,
Out of the core of midnight made our way
To meet the grandiose daybreak far away,

While unknown thousands brushed us and were gone,
Whence, whither, in that night's oblivion.

Oaths, shouts and cries rose o'er the incessant din
Of wheel and hoof, and many a frantic blow.
The dazed beasts battle through that tumult in
The darkness at the driver's lash to win
A goal unknown: nor do the thousands know
The event in course, but likewise blindly go.

After the dramatic and successful attack on the morning of July 18 the batteries of our artillery brigade followed up our infantry in successive exhilarated advances into the open terrain southwest of Soissons during the next few days. There were sporadic resistances of the enemy, and I recall one occasion when our position was too advanced. This was the only time in my artillery experience when I actually heard the zing of German rifle bullets during our action. Their aviation took its toll on some of our batteries. Notable in these days was the extensive use of German guns by our crews which were turned around and their fire with their own ammunition directed with our own at the retreating foe.

In this open warfare in an area long stabilized we overran German positions where, for example, an underground command post had long been furnished with luxurious accommodations—electric lighting, brass beds, fine china, and all the comforts of a secure domicile.

After our infantry had been withdrawn our weary batteries were relieved on July 25. There followed several days of rain-soaked marches and bivouacs. We supposed that we were then to take part in divisional maneuvers. But at a railhead the entire artillery brigade boarded eight separate trains and was transported east to the region of Nancy. This was the most comfortable trip in French boxcars we had known, as there were plenty of cars and a good supply of straw and blankets.

I recall, however, the exasperating difficulties we had in loading our skitterish horses by ramp into their obscure cars. The capacity of the French box-cars was regularly indicated by the notation 8 CHEVAUX— 36 HOMMES. In my journal I took some pleasure in dramatizing the pain-

ful process of persuading our nervous critters to mount the ramp and
occupy their allotted spaces:

> The first horses urged in plunge, kick out and fall-down.
> "Bang! Bang! They're making a noise like a dozen batteries. There
> won't be anything left of this sawed-off freight car!"
> "Whoa! Whoa! Tie the S.O.B.'s in here before they trample me
> to death!"
> "Put a little straw up to 'em. A horse will come out of delirium tre-
> mens for a wisp of hay."
> "As soon as they get done with it, though, they begin to see things."
> Two men come out of the menagerie, pale and limping.
> "That's the way it goes. I was drunk as a cuckoo when I joined this
> man's army."
> "Singing: 'Why didn't we wait to be drafted?'" "Whoa there, you
> _____ brutes! Shut the door on them. They'll all be dead when we
> open it again, anyway."
> "There gotta be three men stay in there with 'em, too."

The regimental history notes that during the first days of supposed
relaxation near Nancy and by the Moselle our brigade held a memorial
service for those who had been lost in the Villers-Cotterets drive. Our
Seventeenth Regiment chaplain, then and after the war, was Ovid Sell-
ars, later like myself a biblical scholar in Chicago—in his case at the
McCormick Seminary. He long continued in this post as a cherished
officer of our postwar regiments and its reunions. Indeed, he was one of
those who wrote the regimental history.

At this point, his record also mentions the great batch of belated letters from the States which were distributed to the men and the eagerness
with which we read them in our pup tents in the green woodland.

Speaking of the chaplain and our memorial service, I have always
been interested to observe the strictness of protocol of liturgy in the
army. The military tradition had its own piety and ethos which was less
that of Church or sect and more that of a greater lodge or fraternal order.
Dogmatic tenets were vague, but the moral and patriotic consensus was
animated by inherited images and models. The army had its own kind

of what we call "civil religion." Related as this was to the issues of war and death it could be taken very seriously as could its rites.

Years later, when our Indian Head Division had a reunion in Des Moines, at the memorial service there was a vigorous objection to the form in which the service was conducted. It was a question of the correct position of the flag during the exercises—on the right or left of the chaplain! The dispute was carried over to the next day. Reference then to the manual of protocol indicated that it was a question of whether a platform had been used in the service. This kind of scruple and reverence lay back of much of the routine commitment of officers and men. My *marraine de guerre*, Blanche Stanley, told me that her father, a major general, at the point of death suddenly sat up and saluted as one meeting his superior after his tour of duty.

At this time when the battery was on reserve near Nancy and the Moselle, it became necessary for me to leave for a long separation for reasons of health. My fatigue after the events of July was evidently deepseated. Though during the first weeks of August I continued with the usual details and missions such as scouring the villages for the officers' mess, I must have had some kind of radical depletion, made up of battle fatigue, sleeplessness, and nervous strain. Duties had to be pursued under a kind of cloud and excessive burden. Apart from those who censored my letters and any routine medical checkup, none could suspect what was a kind of chronic anguish in my condition. The need for a minor operation, namely for circumcision, put me in a hospital, and this apparently drew attention to my more general discomfiture, and I was held over for further observation.

Aug. 1, 1918. Thur. 12 midnight to 1:30 en route with Hdqs Co on road, slept in field. 7:30–12M—on road to our rest-camp (Messein). Billeting till Battery in and located at 7 PM—next canal swimming—Shelter tent pitched—Lending money—Fellows in town after liquor and worse. I bought officers some specialties and found them a Mme to handle their *popote* [officers' field-mess]—a new Chaplain—Let's hope we get a good rest here. Quite a ways to water, tho' . . .

Aug. 2. Day taken up with watering, feeding, grooming, close-order drill, etc. Also I was arranging for officers' mess, buying them eggs, etc. Not much rest. The Dr. is going to see me about circumcision.

Aug. 3–5th—Still at Messein—working with Batty—5 AM to 8 PM—everybody tired—many sighs—Lt. Byars etc. with dysentery-like fever—one fellow pneumonia—chiefs of [gun] sections look dead with fatigue.

Aug. 13 Space line harness cleaning afternoon til 3. B.C. says to take out a horse and go to 9th Infantry Hdqs and Supply to look for "A" Battery horse—small, brown, 15 hands/high, white spot middle forehead—poor condition. "If you don't find him there keep going till you find him." An absurd order . . . I came back after covering the whole 9th Division Hdq—Belleville—Landremont—Hillary—at 7:45 PM dead tired. No horse. . . .

Sec'y Daniels, Hoover etc. and 17 autos passed up yesterday "they say"—Rumored that Wilson over here secretly. First success of Americans attack over. Will it pick up again? I heard our division was going to move a long ways yesterday. Goods marked "Brest" Russia—Italy—States?—where? We are in 1st [?] American Army—just formed.

Relevant to my disability during this period is a letter received from Jules Deschamps about this time. The young Lieutenant, something of an analyst, has been led to identify "les quatre maux du soldat":

Le danger
Le rigueur du régime
La neurasthenie
L'abrutissement.

The soldier no doubt, and cumulatively, suffers all these banes, and these may well penetrate to his deepest levels of fortitude. The list allows for the recurrent unsettling of fear as well as the coercion of authority. Knowing Deschamps one can appreciate his dread of neurasthenia as well as of every kind of coarsening. Of course one question Deschamps is not asking here about the banes, or personal costs, of war is how far the soldier's motivations and incentives fortify his endurance. This links his problem with my own case and many others. Thus one must ask oneself how far battle fatigue or neurasthenia may be due to lack of commitment rather than to sheer extenuation.

In the long interval from mid-August to the end of October, my regiment was at first largely inactive near the Moselle and then took a leading part in the victorious St.-Mihiel attack east of the Meuse. From there it had moved farther west and been engaged in critical battles with the enemy east of the Champagne at Blanc Mont in the Aisne. It was here at Blanc Mont Ridge that after my lengthy displacement I later rejoined my unit, then on the point of being relieved preparatory to the great attack of November 1 in the Argonne which led to the Armistice.

After this overall sketch of my displacements the reader may more easily situate any details I now introduce from my Journal entries from August 16–18 document a few days when we were still near Nancy and the Moselle not long before my hospitalization and separation from the Battery.

Aug. 16 (near Moselle)—I have canvas leggings since this AM. Better for circulation. When is my 9 day furlough coming—Aix? A long talk with Fred Teiderman last night. He doesn't go to town on passes because of temptation. Gave me light on what an extreme temptation it is to the men. Also how hard a time he has with bookwork—worry. He wants to be a driver—private.

Most of my thinking is about my poor health–dislike of work—staleness. Self-reproach and desperation. Why can't they put me into congenial work that won't take the nervous energy so? Etc., etc. But then there is the philosophy of being in such and such a position "by God's will" and make the best of it. Should this preclude efforts to locate oneself more harmoniously?

[Aug. 16] Bought for officers' mess. Lt Groves—Maynard and self after hay for the Battery. Slept awhile in guardhouse for better concealment. This aft[ernoon] whistle at 2:30. "Get towel." Sgt Campbell marched us across canal and we bathed in Moselle . . .

Feeling a lot better, tho' I could sleep 20 hours a day and I groan whenever I get a job.

Finished Merchant of Venice. That great last Act—gave himself up to poetry. Really drama is second to poetry—the ducat-daughter scene invented but not the poetry. Now reading Gt Expectations. I don't write many letters.

Rumors about division being broken up, about Marines going on MP duty at sea coast base. Wharton gone with 5 days rations—to Brest they say . . . Some of division left today and a fellow told me the 17th was left under the command of the relieving 82nd [Div].

Aug. 18—After dinner as it was getting dark—I was walking on the Moselle canal tow-path—I noticed 5 French balloons going up in the dusk with (probably) nets against German airplanes which bombard Nancy every night. I stayed till 10:30 to watch. Almost before it was dark the throbbing hum of the Boche to the north—while they were almost unheard, two signal shrapnels over Frouard.—Then one could hear the horns and sirens at Nancy—12 kilometers away. Lights out. The searchlights played a little but not too much lest they give away the "sausages." The [German] planes tacked back and forth and then droned over my head (bright starlight and full moon) right to Nancy. None seem to have met the nets. A little later there was the winking, winking of shrapnel continuously over Nancy quite low in the sky. Then the detonations. Then more aeroplanes overhead and so on. I heard machine guns in the sky, and saw tracer bullets fired from the ground. The searchlights played a good deal. It got cloudy as I was going home down the road. A single Boche turned—probably for fear of getting lost—and turning overhead let go his cargo where he was. I heard the whirring of the bombs—then the sharp long whistle and expected them anywhere. Great flashes across the valley by the lumber mill. The reports and a great cloud of dust against the hill, plainly visible at night. The Boche then went home and I to bed.

My minor operation took place on August 30 at a time when many units of our division were breaking camp to take part in the St.-Mihiel offensive. A day or two later I, like one of my own earlier patients, was being carried in a speeding, swaying ambulance back to rejoin my battery, though I had set my hopes on being held for a period of rest and observation.

Aug. 30—3:15 PM. . . . Circumcision at noon today by a young Dr—1st Lt. who used to live in Madison [Wisconsin—my birthplace]. Had left Battery Aug 27. Arrived here by Ambulance . . . at Base Hosp. 66 for operation on Aug. 29. Cdn't keep me under the circumstances (rush). The Capt said I could do much more for myself by getting the right mental attitude than they could ever do. En route back alone in flying Ambulance had a mental crisis. It seemed I never would get any strength—and they were rushing me back into that hell of life in the Battery with enthusiasm gone to the last and alone.—When I get back I am decided to try to get into Brigade Hdqs feeling that I will not thus be shirking my call. In the ambulance I thought myself on the point of insanity once or twice. The problem of submission or self-emancipation—"That station in life to which it has pleased God to call us" *VS* extrication from the dwarfting of one's personality.

Sept. 2—Hospital about to move—division moving apparently. If hospital moves before night I will be evacuated to rear and miss the coming drive. If tomorrow I will rejoin Battery here—tho' still incapacitated.

Fortunately for me our unit had already vacated its position, and I was returned to the base hospital where some perceptive medico thought I could well have further attention. After moves to several hospitals and convalescent centers with regimes of rest and recreation I began to feel more like myself. There followed mysterious orders which took me hither and yon, including Lyon and even Marseilles, with sleeping accommodations perhaps on a Red Cross bunk or a waiting room bench.

The army had its reasons for all such strange detours as I was going through. A soldier absent from his unit at the front could only be restored thither by way of some replacement center or assembly point for all those of the same unit.

In my case this led to my arrival at the Le Corneau center.

Sept. 15—To Le Corneau [near Bordeaux] . . . Placed in Hdqs Co—F.A. Replacement Reserve—as casuals—about 500 of us in French thatched barracks but half sleeping outdoors in shelter halves because of Spanish influenza epidemic.

Sept. 25—still here—quarantined for indefinite time with above. Many precautions—600–700 cases out of different batteries of FA in "isolating Barracks"—quite a regular no. of deaths. Camp all sand—little foliage—much rain. A School of fire and aviation camp in neighborhood. Work as orderly at Infirmary, [also] drilling 8:30–11:30–1:30–4:30 with rifles, gas-masks, semaphore, simulated gun drill, ditching and improving tents—Each man has a tent (2 shelter-halves) to himself—and a wooden bunk that raises him 5 inches off the ground—a "tick" full of straw or hay—three blankets and slicker. We non-coms give the drilling—manual of arms. Outside of drill hrs—there is a YMCA bldg with official bulletins (Canteen, movies, French class, religious services, change-money, etc., all closed account of quarantine). The arrival of papers with news of Salonika and Palestine victories at 11 AM. Formal guard mount, band, at officers mess . . . football kicking and baseball throwing once in a while—bathing in dirty creeks outside quarantine.

Two of my letters home describe this period. I wrote on August 31:

Here in the wards is a bunch of fellows, all cheerful, most of whom are here as a result of accidents in their training while in the rear between acts. A left-hander interferes with a right-hander next to him in grenade practice, and a grenade is dropped. Or a motorcycle accident; or an old wound or broken limb from horseback. Every morning the Y.M.C.A. man gives out a franc bar of chocolate and cigarettes; the chaplains bring magazines . . . After lights are out, one can hear groups talking of their experiences and puffing away on their elbows. A motorcycle dispatch rider that morning (the 18th) at Soissons said he was up and down the road just after the doughboys. Said he carried a bucket of water on his handle bars for the many fellows lying at the side of the road who could not be instantly reached by litter-bearers. This fellow is a fluent German speaker and does interpreting at headquarters. Other men in the Engineers, Marines, Infantry tell of experiences in hand-to-hand fighting. The wonder is the richness (mixed with vulgarity), the exact aptness of soldier-slang: the devil's poetry of metaphor, etc. The only theory I can offer is that in a time like this there is a special spirit or gusto that gives all men concerned an epic quality that they don't realize (because of its universality). There is little religion in the armies but one of the most Christian qualities is widely attained among all those who fight and that is humility—a sanity of self-conception that gives a tremendous amount of sincerity and expressiveness.

[From letter dated September 8.] It is taking longer than I thought to get back to the Battery. I was to have gone back September 3 from the field hospital but it moved; therefore I was evacuated to a base hospital way back. We were not accepted by the first two but finally were taken in at a new one any number of kilometers to the rear. There were a great number of long, well aired and well lighted wooden barracks with two rows of shining white hospital beds. And these beds were so soft and cool and the pillows so downy that I nearly forgot myself. Being nearly healed, after one night, they sent me to this convalescent camp, about six kilometers.

Yesterday I was transferred to "C Class" and will soon be on my way back to the battery. I haven't been anywhere nearly so much myself in two years as I was the other day when I got out on that baseball diamond . . .

Carlyle's picture of Odin, the old Norse and Teuton hero-god suggests some interesting things. Germany has a tremendous strength and there must be some relation in it to this old Odin worship. Indeed I think it very likely that she has an element of valor and a fortress-quality a little of which could not do harm to some of the other nations; a Spartan, heroic, giant-like strength, born of whirlwind and darkness which is different from our Anglo-Saxon strength or the French. I verily think that Germany has here a contribution to make to the world even yet, now that the dangers of its abuse have been shown. The rank commercialism that follows this war will have to be tempered by some new quality, some instinct for self-denial and away from luxury, or there will be more trouble!

An interesting corporal here from the mining regions of Kentucky. Has mined in the States and in Peru. He met a Y.M.C.A. woman some months ago over here. She told him she was a student at Harvard on the effect of the climate of the Andean Plateau on the inhabitants. He had lived down there and seen many of the remote villages that she had studied and visited. This fellow is only a boy. Goes about with a pipe, very deliberately. Has a big scar on one side of his face and rather weak eyes. He is anxious for a higher education but for curiosity of knowledge he beats a professor. His talk on the traditions of the Cherokees (from their official records), on the similarity between Mexican and Egyptian sculpture and an interesting argument for the truth of the "Lost Atlantica," of the habits of spiders, etc., is almost weird . . .

One of the fellows told about the Galveston flood; the planned bulwarks; his own break into life by working on the docks with longshoremen and cotton-jammers. What an amount of fine, raw material is going into this war in the ranks. Unschooled, coarse often, but fairly disciplined by home memories—a father or mother, or by a long pull in the early days at work, or by some girl's love often, or by some unknown grade school teacher. Or the imagination has been captured in boyhood by some Decoration Day ceremony. Most of it is pretty well submerged by the recklessness that they like to put on. And there is a tendency to assume a crowd-spirit with much grumbling and worse sometimes. But getting at each man alone, or getting the crowd in good spirit, you have a promise for America that is immeasurable. To handle the element is required the ability to look for the best in them, to expect it, to show one's liking for them when at their worst. This is the officer's job. Prince Hal put it:

I see you stand like greyhounds in the slips,
Straining upon the leash—you noblest English, etc.

Rest Camp, September 11

I left the convalescent camp yesterday, the captain doctor pro-

nouncing me a "splendid physique." A party of 17 of us under a
sergeant took the train to this camp, whence we go to various replacement camps according to the division we belong to . . .

Traveling about in the rear this way one is astonished at the way
Americans have taken possession of French [scene and] life. Indeed a woman who gave two of us a little supper of eggs and French
fried (*frits*) potatoes asked me in perfect naiveté if I did not think
the Americans would *own France* after the war. She seemed not
to abhor the possibility. In their village they have lost 100 men,
practically all, and they seem to doubt whether France will have
sufficient men and masculinity to prosper after the war. The daughter of the house who made our omelet for us had lost her brother
the month before. They must feel a peculiar grief in losing one who
has survived four years only to fall at the moment of victory. When
French people tell me of the ruin and bankruptcy of their country, I
try without too much forcing to suggest that it is the "valeurs spiri-
tuels" that count. They take this with a kind of brooding skepticism.
They have suffered too much to feel the pride of the sacrifice.

Well, this town, for instance, has been made into a tremendous
railroad center—that's why we were sent here, because we can go
anywhere from here, by American engines no doubt. Through the
countryside one sees American camps, hospital, training, rest,
every kind of camp. On the lines one passes "gorgeous" American
hospital trains, and troop trains from which the boys shriek and
whistle to each other above the noise of the train. Every town has its
M.P.'s at the station, etc. Really, our American energy and abandon
intoxicate one. If only one could be sure it is due to the integrity
of our national life rather than just to the youthfulness itself of our
nation.

The French woman told me that there were Russian troops in
their neighborhood when the revolution began. These killed a
couple of officers and put on the red cockade. They used to come
into the town every night and try to break into the houses and to
knock on the doors when the men of the house were all away at the
front. She shuddered as she told me how they used to lock up regularly at 8 p.m. When it was announced that the Americans were

coming to that town the women all got together full of forebodings and said, "Ils seront comme les Russes," and they were frightened. The first day the Americans were there they stole around to each other's kitchens and said in a whisper, "Mais, ils ne sont pas si méchants." The next day they said, nothing horrible having happened, "Mais, ils sont trés gentils." And the third day and afterwards they quite adored the American boys. Only making the reserve that of course everywhere there are to be found a few exceptions.

After being in several hospitals I found myself, as noted, in a replacement camp. Here, however, hundreds of "casuals" and replacements were then trapped by the grave influenza epidemic of the season which had led to many fatalities so that we were not allowed for some weeks to leave the camp and thus spread the infection. Thus it was only near the end of October that I was able to get a pass with a few others and regain the sector of my regiment and resume my duties. Here I would find that I had been transferred from A Battery to our headquarters company. This meant that I henceforward had much more congenial tasks of desk work, map tracing, and measurement in the office with the colonel and the adjutant. In fact, it may have been a matter of compunction which led my officers to this reassignment. They must earlier have had inklings of my exhaustion, perhaps in the course of censoring my letters. That my services as corporal had not been as ill-suited as I thought became evident when our Second Battalion requested my transfer to their staff. Our then regimental commander told me of this, and as he hung up the phone said, "What will they want next!" But first more about the replacement camp.

Located at Le Corneau in a waste of sand and pines south of Bordeaux, the replacement camp was an astonishing sort of army base—all the more so because of the influenza epidemic which trapped so many hundreds of us at the time. The administration had both to provide for those who were infected and to keep the rest of us busy with drills and make-work assignments. One of my tasks was to escort newly infected men with their belongings to their ward in the crowded infirmary area. Fortunately, I remained immune myself.

Many of those who like myself were quarantined here were from various U.S. units engaged at the front, but many also had just arrived from the States still awaiting training in France. Thus my contacts here as well as my displacements thither and back afforded a rich experience of our American involvement in the war apart from actual service at the front.

Le Corneau marked the farthest point of my travels, for it was 700 miles back to my battery and my new duties.

Le Corneau near Bordeaux, September 27

Today makes a month since I left the battery and have been in the rear. This is a camp in the sand. It has been used by Russians, French and no doubt Senegalese, etc. Most of the men here are drafted soldiers. They have had very little training. They will be sent as replacements to organizations in the service, but only so fast as they can be trained by the experienced men they will mix with. The men like myself who have been at the front and come back here via hospitals, schools, etc. will return to their old "outfits." The others listen to our stories open-mouthed . . .

At headquarters there is a band. When they are rehearsing for funerals they really do make agreeable selections—classical music. After 4:30 there is formal guard mount with band; or the band plays at the officers' mess outdoors and the men gather about it; or the Y.M.C.A. is open for extempore music and writing letters. All its other activities are closed on account of quarantine.

I have made a very interesting acquaintance in this fellow Fettner, the mining engineer, who wants to go to Sheff [Yale's Engineering program]. He was born in the great side-eddy of America, among the "Kentucky whites," and as a child remembers the large-scale feuds in open defiance of justice. He remembers the Court House of his own town being riddled with rifle holes. He rather resents the fact that the rest of the states criticize the frequency of "ambushes" in these hills, and asks why that should be accounted worse than shooting men when they are asleep in bed, as in New York. He thinks their method is more legitimate. He says all these ignorant people need is to be taken out of their environment and given an *idea*. He cites some John M——— who went out from these hills, a sheepish fellow, and died a millionaire. His own father, I gather, was something of a speculator; lost everything. All he has said of his mother is that the only reason for which he regrets not having a commission is his mother. They wired him to be at Officers' School in the States, but he arrived from Peru a day late. He has a very large capacity for useful knowledge. He learned all his mining by taking hold of a foreman's job; or chemist's job or assayer's job quite ignorant of the work, but studying day and night until he had it.

September 29

Every day's paper brings in reports of new victories in Palestine, Serbia, Lorraine; at St. Quentin and Cambrai. The American First Army in which our division is, is right near my old Argonne roads in this new attack. Yesterday the French paper had the news of Bulgaria's move for peace. Another year ought to finish things up.

October 6

Your wandering boy is still immured way back here behind the lines. Meanwhile the *"bataille de la France"* (as the correspondents call it) draws to a close and *"la bataille des nations"* begins. I speculate as to whether the fates deem me unworthy of participating in so great an action. I don't know whether our army corps is engaged now west of the Meuse or not. We did our work in June and July when these now fighting were in training. But it should be our turn again. The Argonne would seem like old times to me. Much of the staleness which made me unfit for good service when I left the Battery has worn off . . .

I note with amusement that among the nicknames one gives strangers in the army—"Bud," "Shorty," etc—I usually get "Big Boy." It doesn't seem to me that I am taller than when I left, but I may have grown some.

Today I got a French paper, and amid all the good news of the military events read that Germany, Austria and Turkey follow Bulgaria and ask President Wilson for armistice. I don't think it will be accepted yet. The Germans must be clearly defeated, if not humiliated. This will take another year's campaign. There is a possibility, however, that President Wilson will rely upon the guarantees of a society of nations for the insurance against new aggression rather than on a complete military victory. The French editorials betray a venomous hatred of the enemy, now that they have the upper hand at last. This is increased by the manner in which the Germans conduct their retreat across France. The French are a bit jealous that the Central Powers address their offer to President Wilson. Yet they need our army to carry out whatever retribution they desire to execute on Germany.

[Journal, Le Corneau, early October]

The drafted soldiers here in camp as replacements—who have had only a dull experience on top of their first homesickness— really exhibit blueness over the failure of the peace proposition. They really hope not to go to the front. The gas mask drill and lectures, and the overdrawn stories of men from the front, have made them fainthearted. It almost amounts to cowardice.

Movies and YM entertainments—boxing, wrestling outside on "ring" and screen. Lady singers' entertainment spoiled by the vulgar and cheap remarks thrown at them from the men. A very unfortunate thing happened near this camp a short time ago. One fellow who talks French said that many of the French think of the American soldiers as being like the Germans in the way of barbarianism. There was a hanging here just before I arrived, but it seems not to have done much good.

On first reading this in my journal I thought that hanging would not have been a proper penalty at that time in a court-martial proceeding as compared, for example, with a firing squad. I have been undeceived about this. But there still remains the unlikeliness of this extreme resort and the quandary of the whole situation. Evidently there had been disorder, drunkenness, and disobedience some time back among undisciplined American elements. The low morale and disaffection of many in this transient and dismal detainment could have occasioned the disparagements of French observers and actions which called for drastic penalty by the military. In any case this situation calls attention to the general problem of morale among some of the elements in the American contingents.

[Journal, early October, continued]

One finds more and more that there is no man in the army who does not talk interestingly on some topic. Tonight a squat young corporal whom I had taken for an 18 year old—I find has been married over a year. Lives in Portland, Me. Has been on "the road" with tobacco and groceries for 6 yrs in Maine, NH and V't. Told me all about Pres. Wilson's home [summer White House] in Cornish, N.H. The Poorest Pres we ever had. Announced he cd not keep up receptions, etc. Had 3 official autos and 4 chauffeurs [hardly used] at Cornish. "House cd. not have cost over 25,000" One could not help feeling proud.

Fettner wants to adopt a French child. Wants to raise Angora goats in the Andes. Wants to tour the principality in the Pyrénées between France and Spain. Wants to start a revolution in central South America among the savage tribes. "There's lots of money in it," he commented in reverie. "A second Warren Hastings, heh?" Wants to go into western China. Wants to write up the spiders in his home county that write English on their webs. Wants to see numbers of Ford cars with blinded turrets and hard-rubber wheels and machine guns precede the cavalry into the open country behind the lines. Every conversation he has a dozen new ideas. He got the scar on his face in a fight with a Negro on a r.r. car. He told of a palmreader who told him the story afterwards.

The next two long letters to the family cover the 700-mile journey back to my battery.

October 17

I believe that this is the first Sunday I've missed writing you in two years; it is now Thursday. On the way back they put us in for 24 hours with a great crowd of casuals and replacements in the shelter-tent city in the rain. Saturday night we were loaded on box cars, though we of the very first divisions got a second class coach.

Eight of us had a compartment. But with our dough boy packs and full equipment it was pretty crowded at that. Fettner and myself were together as usual. Then there was a comical sergeant and five others who pretended they were corporals if there was any work for privates, or privates if any work for corporals. The next car held the officers who made great efforts to keep the fellows on the train at stops, none of which succeeded. Once a day rations were issued to the sergeant in charge of each car and he distributed to the compartments (or 40 men in box cars). We had for four days nothing but corn-wooly [army beef], tomatoes, beans, all cold; but we did have beautiful bread. Yes, one-half can of jam a day in each compartment. A four days' trip across France—one more new route for me, including the Limoges country. But the nights were fierce. It would have been better in the box cars. For our legs were so cramped, etc., that we could not lie down or only half so, and we would wake every hour with our foreheads frozen from the window pane, or neck warped, or a leg paralyzed. I remember W———— of old SSU2 [Ambulance Section #2] woke up one night between Reugny and Paris with his head in a major's lap . . . The events of the day were the cold meals, the officers' encounters with offenders. The funniest thing to me, constantly repeated, was the derision with which the whole trainload would greet M.P.'s or S.O.S. [Service of Supply] men, or other men of the rear. Of course we were all old-timers— out of the hospital and seasoned in wars out-of-time. So wherever one or more of these above mentioned greenhorns were sighted, roars would go up from the whole train of swinging legs and outstretched necks thus, "Who's going to win the war?" Chorus: "The M.P.'s" Or (when the news of Germany's first capitulation came), "Who won the war?" Chorus: "The National Guard," or "The Transportation Department." Or they would yell out: "What are you doing to win the war, you bomb-proofers?" Or any number of imprecations and jeers—mostly in good humor. It's surprising how a bunch of fellows who have been at the front are proud of it, and how superior they feel to anyone that hasn't. It's the old poilu-gendarme conflict.

Once a day or oftener we'd come to some "Coffee Station." The men lighted little fires often at the halts to warm their corned beef or toast bread. The news of course just at this time was of first interest. French soldiers would yell at us "Fini la guerre" and others, "Vous êtes trop tard" (thinking we had just come over—an insult), or, "Might as well turn 'round." It was quite an experience.—What bothered me was the lawlessness of the men. Incidents of breaking open wine casks, stealing crates of fruit from mail cars, etc. One time at a café where I tried to get a paper, the mistress had just been robbed before her face of some 30 or 40 francs' worth of liqueurs. Without encouraging the liquor traffic, I hope, I led her to the lieutenant, interpreted, tried to help them find the robbers, and probably was generally disliked for it. No result . . .

Here we are, almost at our Division Headquarters. On the way here we had to change trains with a long interval at my old Ste. Ménéhould. I walked for four miles to the old ambulance camp with a poignant sensation. The village, the site of the parking, the billets we had—everything was just the same, except that there was a truck section instead of an ambulance section. The same old hospital was there where I had so often unloaded my *blessés*, except there were strangers going about the old business and Americans working with the French. Then I felt like a pioneer and could have haughtily proclaimed my priority. The carpenter's family called my name out when I entered to ask if by chance they remembered my face, and gave me some hot coffee. We talked of Harmon Craig, who was such a favorite with the children of that family, and who was killed two weeks after I left. Then I went up the hill and looked down on what is to me the most beautiful view in France [at Clanémont], where I had driven so many times up and down; and now I saw it new, for it is autumn and these forests are ablaze with any number of colors. I haven't had such a tug at my heart-strings in a long time. All this region is way behind the lines now.

October 20, 1918. I am back at the echelon of the battery—the battery itself being in firing position in a momentary lull. But it's the front again and the familiar scenes and sounds are anyway welcome.

We are in a village plastered with German signs . . . Well, the old avalanche has begun to gather speed at last. Germany got a beating on the field. Then seeking to even up by diplomacy she exposed herself to some fearful blows from the President. No doubt she will fight obstinately for some time. One hardly sees how our advantage can be turned into a real rout of the enemy. The soldiers frankly admit they were disappointed that the first German capitulation was not grasped and an armistice inaugurated. They say it is "dur" or "tough," but they trust the leaders as seeing the issues more clearly than they, and are willing to make it a "no-stop winter" or whatever Marshal Foch wants. I ought to correct and say that there were lots of soldiers who have seen clearly all the time the impossibility of trusting the German promises. Civilians must realize though that even these swiftest victories are heart-breaking efforts for the troops and sacrifice is as hard in victory as in defeat. The last news is of the fall of Ostend, Lille and Courtrai. That is a conception of genius, that of the "implacable pursuit," the no-let-up, when it is actually embodied in deed. Foch is said to be a strategist of the psychological type—a religious man. He fights with men's faiths and feeds that faith with the application and disposition of his own will.

The thing that awes a man about this war is the infinitude of materials and engines and other forms of supply. How can man himself have delivered all this through hundreds of miles of entanglement—inexhaustible ammunition, big things, little things. It seems as though gods have set the stage and as though gods hold their rods over the river courses and chains of hills and forested regions, saying "Thus far," etc.

Later—Thursday. Am up on my second story bunk while a poker game goes on below (over 100 francs changing hands on a single play). I am working quite carefully on the *L'Ancien régime* (Taine) and get so fascinated with it that I don't know for hours that I am reading French.

We are 10 kilometers from the front lines here, but the barrages we get here in the dawn, and sometimes (as now) in the afternoon, are formidable. It gives one a sense of the perverse endurance in the enemy. If I could only explain the strong sense that comes over one of the personality of the evil we are fighting. The Personal Devil: the Unseen Powers of the Air—a superhuman deviltry of conception, a never failing truth-to-type in action. We men are the tools with which greater beings fight each other.

There is a long tradition that combatants in war mythologize it and ascribe its course to higher powers. This naturally includes identifying the foe and his assaults with supernatural and maleficent agencies.

My pretentious assessment of France in 1918 no doubt reflects one vein of French nationalism. But as with other parties to the European conflict, then and later, they should be balanced by a more searching appraisal. France from of old and throughout its history had its commitment to internationalism, and one need only mention Aristide Briand and Jean Monnet as witnesses in our period. It was above all the intellectual role of France's leading writers in this time of political and cultural crisis which helped us transcend either outworn patriotisms or the false internationalisms of totalitarianism.

These next two letters cover more of my return to the battery.

October 27

Day before yesterday a message came for me to report from the battery echelon over to headquarter's office. The adjutant, Lieutenant Hendron, took me out in the hall and said he was looking for somebody to take Sergt. Vaughan's place in the orienting work. Sergt. Vaughan has left now for Saumur—the Officers' Training School. The adjutant asked me if I'd had surveying, mechanical drawing, trigonometry, etc. When I said "no" he pondered; then said he'd give me a trial. Told Sergt. Vaughan to give the day to me, and show me the work and equipment. It seems the job is a sinecure. As the lieutenant said when he told me to report over for the work with my equipment next morning, it will give me an opportunity to study artillery, and see it from the inside. For I work in the office of the regimental sergeant major, and all "dope"—past, present and future—pass through there. Besides I have charge of all the maps, and see every sort of document.

The principal task is this: before an operation a chart comes here from brigade headquarters, with the "missions" [targets, etc.] of our regiment marked out on it. This has to be traced by me for the battalions on tracing paper with the co-ordinates marked so they can refer it right to their battle maps. It has to be done quickly, but it is very easy. Then I have to care for the maps and charts and orienting documents, and be ready to supply any one needed to the colonel at a moment's notice . . . Best of all there is no detail under me, or horse to care for, or rigid schedule. Yet I realize how profoundly ignorant I am of the whole background of orienting, artillery mathematics, etc. Worst of all one can't learn these things out of a book. The formulas, instruments, methods avoid one's grasp unless actually handled. Therefore, I can't aspire to the rank of sergeant held by the man before me. But I'm working 10 or a dozen hours a day and will pick up something. From 7:30 P.M. on I read my "Barnaby Rudge" or Taine. I am getting books from the army library at Paris for the artillery study.

Properly speaking, this is the regimental headquarters. The colonel, adjutant, and several officers for telephone, ammunition, observation, etc. About 50 men with 20 horses for the "details," for telephone, wireless, reel cart, kitchen, orderlies, etc. One lives generally in a town—without the regime of "calls," "inspection," etc., and with privileges of being near stores and canteens, Y.M.C.A., chaplain, dentist, the official communiqués from the wireless, the official time from Eiffel, etc.

November 4

Here we are located in a house the Germans were in almost no time ago, and still we have to move up the third time to catch up with them. All my maps, tracing paper, etc. are laid out ready to use, so soon as an order comes in. I had to trace out the firing charts for the different batteries when the [present] big drive was about to reopen. I knew about it all before it began and it was surely a barrage. I went outside when it started and as far as one could see either way there was the continuous roar and flashes, hour after hour until light and then on till after midday. When one lay down indoors the guns sounded like the sucking and ebbing and swirling of a whirlpool. At such times one feels with uncomfortable clearness that sense of awe towards the future. History making itself, now, now at this ordinary night and dawn and day and in this ordinar[il]y grand landscape. One comes too close to the divine plan and sees Castor and Pollux fighting over the Roman phalanxes at Lake Regulus, palpably.

I guess now no one will deny that ours (Second) is the best division in the army. Our doughboys and Marines have made child's play of what has stopped all the other divisions and even Frenchmen.

The common expression among the men nowadays is "I guess there must be a war on somewhere." This comes out whenever a shell whistles somewhere or a barrage breaks out on the horizon. And because there have been so many rumors of armistice. Again one fellow says, "The war's over!" "Yes, all over Europe."

The colonel of the regiment (in whose office I work) is now a taciturn grim fellow but exceedingly courteous. K[een] and A[llen], who work with me, tell me of the time when (now Brig-Gen) Col. Bowley used to rule the office. They say he was emitting sparks all the time (reminded one of a dynamo), whirling around all the time. They say the men had the time of their life listening to him. He used to go wild because the French would limit his ammunition in a quiet sector. He would come into the office in the morning and say, "Well, B——, what can we shoot at this morning? We've got to shoot something up. B——, find me something to shoot at." (Capt. B—— being the adjutant). They said that in the short walk to breakfast Bowley would be giving orders to B—— over his shoulder and by the time he had reached the door he'd have three or four "parties" started (a "party" is a little bombardment or attack).

I portrayed this colorful and vociferous Major Bowley when he commanded our regiment just before and at the time when our battery galloped in to take up its position near Belleau Wood in the first days of June. Here is a good example of the way officers built up a personal legend of themselves which played no small part in their authority over the men in critical situations. Discipline and morale were strongly affected by such human factors as pride in one's squad or battery and its officers with the associated emulation vis-á-vis other competing units. It may seem paradoxical, but artillerymen and Marines risked their lives for the reputation of their outfits as well as for the objectives in the field of battle.

The adjutant now is a big fellow, a kind of business-man soldier. He's my boss as the Colonel is his. Then there's the Sergeant Major of the regiment who has his field desk and type-writer, who never pays any attention to anybody. His motto is, "It isn't what you can do but what you can get away with."He is reading my *Cloister and the Hearth*. I finished "Barnaby Rudge." We hit the road every day or every other day. All our rolls and packs go on a wagon and we walk behind the "radio wagon." It is an immense relief, and I feel almost a slacker when I see those ammunition trains with the men all mud and curses, or listen from my warm bed to the endless line outside in the dark and the rain.

It doesn't seem as though the war could last much longer. Whether on the Meuse or the Rhine, anywhere, an allied attack can take five or six kilometers in a day under any circumstances. And the difference in the scales increases daily. This must be evident to the Germans, and if they have a trace of their former craftiness left they will appease us now at any cost.

Since October 2, my regiment had been engaged in a costly but successful drive in the Blanc Mont sector. In my new assignment at regimental headquarters at Dricourt I was immediately involved in firing missions and barrages which led to further advances of our infantry. We were then relieved, however, preparatory to our share in the imminent decisive attack of the Allies further east, in the Argonne Forest, on November 1.

Oct. 29. Tuesday A.M. (march delayed causa poor condition battery's horses) to Servon . . . The news these days exciting and papers late. We put up the radio to catch the 3 PM Eiffel report. Mornings freezing cold.

Oct. 30. Wednesday 12 N to 8 or 9 P.M. march (good weather—exciting cross roads—heavy traffic—like before Soissons drive) Camp in field and shacks near Exermont—5 kils from front . . . Drive not 31st after all but next morning Fri–Nov 1st at 5:30.

[*Oct. 31*] I worked on the tracings for the batteries from 4 PM—Nine hour rolling barrage—2 hr preparation. We knew the "H hour," etc. etc. Saw charts of divisional lane with 1, 2, 3rd objectives.—

Work over at 9 P.M. Went to sleep in the office of self and Sgt and Major with that sense of awe towards the future—the realization of the men out getting ammunition in the dark, the traffic at cross-roads with the occasional shells—the infantry plodding slowly up to their places before all—the tanks ready etc.

[*Nov. 1*] Of course at H–2 hrs (3:30) I woke up to the terrific barrage. To the right and left as well as in front the formidable roll of detonations and echoes with the heavy undertone of the barrage in sectors far away. There was a rumor that the attack was to be general from sea to Switzerland—and there was a rather aweful sense of the burden of the future—about to be delivered and possibly of such gigantic proportions—and yet all unguessed. The oppressive sense—almost sight of history writing itself in the minutes of the night and day in the coming of the light of this, this ordinary day in this, this barren environment. It made one dizzy. So the hours went by and the firing lifted until the thirsted-for news came in in various rumors of success (the day's objective was 8½ or 9 kilometres away), prisoners taken, objectives gained, etc.—also wounded in Ambulances or walking. It was all like a great engineering problem seen from the office—the allotments of tasks, the laying of plans with factors all more or less scientifically estimated—and the result almost scientifically sure.

Plans made for wounded, roads, traps, advance, relief, rations, all type-written out and arranged for long before.—A proposition like Panama Canal or a big tunnel.

Nov. 2. Today—end of 2nd day in Landres—St George—ahead 8 kils (last night) but no advance here today because the division on our left (80th) of all—was belated and found heavy resistance. Now at 6:30 in a no-rain-proof shack full of half plugged shrapnel holes the Col—Major—Adjutant are talking about ammunition and we (Keen—Allen—self) are waiting for the "operation chart" for tomorrow's attack (presumable)

—Just this minute as I put this in my pocket an officer came into the office: "Well, I've got good news for you, Col. We've lost contact with the Germans. They're in full retreat. The General wants all the horses left up at the front. He's going to send us a battalion or two with the light artillery," etc, etc, etc.

Fosse—Tue. Nov 5, '18. That turned out to be wrong. The Germans were resisting. Instead of a mere march, the operation for the 3rd became an attack. Hdqs moved to Bayonville—and on the 4th to Fosse—the infantry being at Beaumont and the river on 5th. The weather is so bad that the ammunition cannot come up. Last night clear—and the Boche were bombing all about these villages—few here if any—but an allied 9″ in the neighborhood kept us awake— us and the window frames.

A two story house—Office and officers' bed room and kitchen downstairs. Men upstairs in bunks. No work except pasting maps and tying up bundles. Keen (Detroit—Ann Arbor Freshman— no trade) is good with the pencil and has made a sign (HQ—17th F.A.). Allen (U. of Washington—engineer—father Y.M.C.A. Seattle) graduated a celluloid ruler for the colonel (Ralph Harry Dunlap—taciturn—low voiced—rational). Adj—Lt Hendren— telephone Sgt Harding—radio Sgt Coble—O'Hara—Red Allen, etc. etc. Lts France, Douglas, Jumper.

The Kaiser has resigned. Turkey has capitulated. The last paper says that Austria has been informed of the conditions of an armistice. Germany will soon petition for the same information. Whether the mighty revolution in the world initiated by these four years of war is already sufficiently impelled—or whether it will take an "era of 25 years of war" and revolution to effect the same remains to be seen. As far as America and Europe are concerned, it looks as though the Mighty Voice Rev. 21:5 ["Behold, I make all things new."] were passed in this brief time. Russia—the Balkans—the Slavs—Manchuria may be only started on a course of upheaval.

The entries in my journal covering Armistice Day and the days immediately preceding it expose many facets and contingencies, often trifling, of the war zone at this climactic moment, at times clouded with confusion.

Beaumont (on the Meuse above Verdun)—Nov. 13, 1918. Saturday night, Nov 9, The regimental Post of Command being at the Le Forge farm and the Batteries being near Beaumont (which was then much bombarded) a party was to have been pulled off. But it was countermanded for some unknown reason.

Next day—Sunday—we got papers for the 8th—saying that Foch had given the German envoys the terms of an armistice with a 72 hour period to answer in.

I hung around the Radio room and translated all the French we could pick up—a few references to certain articles of the armistice—Eiffel tower communiqués and POZ (Berlin) code—and some German. There were rumors around that the armistice had been signed. Fellows reported seeing formations and sudden cheering in other outfits. Our officers were getting in reports from Brigade all the time but sat tight in their warm room and office and never made a step to inform the men. Even when they knew absolutely that the armistice was a fact they didn't tell us in a clear and certain way. One officer told one of the fellows he was working with in an ambiguous sort of way. We didn't know till 5 or 6 hours after they did—and then it wasn't their fault. Another outfit had posted the news immediately for the sake of the men.

Our bunch wasn't particularly demonstrative, tho' they understood well it meant peace. They kept remarking for the next few hours and days how strange the absolute silence on the horizon was.

It was told us by the Marines and infantry that the Germans were a lot more tickled than we were. They threw down their gas-masks, helmets, etc. Some were seen up in the tops of trees from our side of the Meuse brandishing their guns and shouting gleefully in our direction. Some Americans had bon-fires the night of the 11th and 12th and let off their spirits with hand-grenades and "potato mashers."

Newton of "A" Battery said that they heard another outfit suddenly burst out cheering Monday morning the 11th ("A" Battery connected by runner not telephone then). He said he "knew then the armistice had been signed or that they were giving out a sack of Durham,"—but they only heard to be sure quite a lot later.

Today in Beaumont the 9th Infantry (2nd Div) Band has played in front of the church and town hall. A quite interesting feeling of victory in all the faces and lightheartedness. Also a new step-up in discipline—care of equipment—as tho' we were going back to the army in time of peace. Town chock full of soldiers (2nd Division) and officers—a few French soldiers and a very few civilians. Men billeted all about town. In this house German and French papers and books lying about when we came in. Upstairs the floors a heap of rubbish and children's toys, etc. (All impregnated with sneezing and tear gas—I wondered what it was that made me sneeze so.) A shell hole in the roof up there.

Keen, Allen, Cpl Arendt in here. Put up stoves. Today all working on reorganization, rechecking materiel, re-equipment. Rumors [we] go to Strassburg. Cigarettes and 2 cookies given out at lunch today. A commissary in town—all sold out. No YMCA yet. Rec'd Gibbon and Franklin from father. Reading Dombey and Son and "Amateur Philosopher" by Grabo.

For a concluding contemporary testimony to the import of the Armistice I turn to a letter from Blanche Stanley, as she describes what she calls the victory atmosphere of the overwhelming demonstration in Paris on November 10, which was by chance Alsace-Lorraine Day in the French calendar.

Sunday, Alsace-Lorraine day, was one never to be forgotten. Just at the right moment, I ran into a friend whose office is in the Hotel Regina and what a view I had, from her room in the top, just over the Jeanne d'Arc Statue! The rue de Rivoli was black with the crowd as far as the eye could reach in both directions, and a dozen or more airplanes were circling, spiralling and darting overhead, in all directions. But there was nothing—there has been nothing yet, for thrills—like the sound! It almost made me able to grasp for a fraction of a second, now and then, what has happened. Instead of staying on the balcony, I preferred to stay in the room, shutting out all else—alone with the roar—unceasing steady deep and calm— from that ocean of so tragically paid joy. Above it, the voices of the children, and through it the boom of the canon, and the whir of the airplanes overhead. In listening, one could grasp things far beyond ordinary comprehension—it seemed the joy of the blessed—a gladness that could last for ever.

The jubilation borne on this surf of sound rising from the multitudes in the streets and the Place de la Concorde—which had in it an aspect of the seraphic—was for something more than the recovery of France's lost provinces.

If the sense of relief brought to the combatants by the Armistice was haunted by a sense of insufficiency and something lacking, it was not because some supposedly more sweeping retribution had not been carried through. It was rather a testimony to the depths of the issues of the war which had come home to the peoples in the agonies of this long ordeal and which still had no answer. This dissatisfaction, no doubt, anticipated the sequel of new disorders which led to World War II, but also reflected an outlook which imposed new demands on our entire period. The complacent premises of a settled society had been undermined, and we knew that we needed an armistice in the aggressions and conflicts of our peacetime existence as well as the one we had attained.

Along with the prose entries in my journal from the time of the Armistice there is one in verse which conveys the conflicting perspectives and passions of that turning-point as many felt them. This poem, prompted by reports of shallow and tasteless celebrations at home, envisages our imminent occupation on the Rhine and the convening of the Peace Conference at Versailles. As its title suggests, its plea may be taken as voicing the goals of history then in the making and the chastened temper even of the victors.

November 11, 1918

Our country, O America, thy sons
Marching to hold an alien land in gage
Conjure thee, hold no revels on the stage
Of tragedy. Mock not the dead. The guns
Are still, the world's pain cries the louder. Now
That fruit of time that raged so to the birth
Comes to delivery, and the wracked earth
Faints, and the lingering dead pause to mark how
The thoughts of many hearts shall be revealed,
Jealous of all their blood-bought testament.
The world's an amphitheatre; Versailles
'Twixt quick and dead dictates a century.
Shall New York flaunt while London's chimes are pealed?
Hold revelry while Paris keeps a Lent?[6]

With these reminiscences and evocation of the Armistice in prose and verse, at the front and in Paris, I conclude my narrative. After our batteries and regiment were motorized we moved across the Rhine. Two recollections of this sequel, however, relate directly to the issues of the war.

One has to do with our relations to the enemy. We were first billeted for a time in Bendorf on the east bank of the Rhine. Here we were strictly warned against "fraternizing with the Germans." Some of us were housed in the home of a baker, and as it was the Christmas season our "hosts" included us in a party for the festive occasion. German *Gemütlichkeit* took precedence over protocol. Since sugar had long been severely rationed we found ways to supplement their meager supply out of our army stores. Thus our host, the baker, and his motherly wife were able to serve the *Küchen* which were so essential a part of our entertainment.

But for us the significance of the Armistice was specially dramatized as we took over the massive fortress of Ehrenbreitstein looking down on Coblenz and the Rhine, with the Stars and Stripes floating high overhead. This immense fortification dating to many periods had gates and walls up to eight feet thick, and our squad rooms were like dungeons. As we surveyed the storied Rhineland and its past from this eminence, we could not but recognize that here surely was a testimony to and a vindication of our New World involvement in the destinies of our surpassing European heritage.

The issues left unresolved at the time of the Armistice still had their background in Europe's long history, and my rehearsal of aspects of the war years will have illustrated these tensions in the ongoing disorders of our whole period. But also—as I have suggested in my dedication to David Jones—there are ancient pledges and auguries of vindication in the historical struggle against the powers of darkness.

✳ ✳ ✳

Epilogue

I recognize that there are many aspects of the war which receive little or no attention in this book. Since the narrative is linked with my own involvement the earlier phases of the long conflict are passed over. But this also means that the bitter and controversial annals of 1914 and 1915 and the fearful losses associated with trench warfare and the great attacks of that period do not come into my picture. Indeed, the hostilities portrayed here are those involving the artillery and the ambulance service, not the infantry. Nevertheless, experience of the Great War was in some respects indivisible, and we have our testimony to add to that of others.

Retrospective reflections on and assessments of the Great War have, of course, varied with the interests of the parties involved, and these interests have responded to changing factors in the public scene. At the time of the Armistice, as the solemn jubilation in Paris testifies, the reaction points to a deep aspiration of the peoples for a concord long associated with the travail in the annals of Europe. This also carried with it the imperative institutionalization of the dream at Versailles.

I look on my informal American journal as reflecting the same impersonal expectation. Here were events reporting themselves. The title I gave to an earlier publication was "At the Nethermost Piers of History: World War I, A View from the Ranks." I had in view the deeper operations of historical forces.

Another retrospect, this time for a shocked appraisal of the war, goes back to the cruel disenchantments of its beginnings but grew especially in England after the war so as to eclipse all considerations save of the hecatombs of the slain. The "old men" of Europe had ordered its youth to slaughter each other one by one on a barren field. Or Abraham had refused to offer the victim provided in place of Isaac and again called for the death of a generation.

This postwar disparagement of the conflict coincided with the more general de-romanticizing of all things martial, their rituals and symbols ("no more parades"), and extended to a cynicism as regards patriotism, heroism, and sacrifice. In this climate of opinion any due appraisal of the war was thwarted from the start. At most, communities lamenting mutilated shrines and bereaved mourners could turn to religious consolations as in the case of Benjamin Britten's moving *War Requiem* for the restoration of Coventry Cathedral. But here was no wrestling with the historical and political antecedents of the costly drama.

A further setting for reappraisal of the war emerged in the twenties with the pressing vogue of visits and pilgrimages to the battlefields. The legendary prestige of such sites of utter devotion and suffering as those associated with Ypres and the Menin Gate, with Verdun and the Fort de Douaumont, could not be denied. A deeper awareness of the war and its import diffused itself.

An editorial written by my father in the twenties reflects on this phenomenon.

It is a wholesome thing for the peoples to keep such memories alive. The war was too vast to be digested in the doing. The effect of an important event in an individual's life only begins with the event itself. His slow reaction and interpretation of it are equally important. So with nations. Peoples must hold their past and present together to understand themselves and their duty . . . The indications are that the temporary period of war-nausea and reaction are drawing to a close.

We are recognizing that the World War was the knot in which were focused not only the threads of the Nineteenth Century but also of the Twentieth. It was not only the retribution for the past but the Open Sesame for the future, so that in the passion and emotion that accompany these great hours of solemnization, as at Ypres, we find men sensing obscurely the world import of what they are evoking. The war was one of these fundamental throes of humanity which escape the analysis of the tactician and the expert, and even of the statesman. The common man feels the surprising, the spiritual element, and these pilgrimages and memories help to bring it out more clearly.

Here on this band of territory from the sea to Switzerland the drama was carried through that has made all other history ancient beside it. By this expiation the crowned heads tumbled, and the map was changed. From it a new diplomacy has issued. Nations were there so tortured that they speak a soberer and more solemn language and are disturbed by a more provocative conscience.

It is the myth-making faculty which lies behind our cult for holy places and pilgrimages. Fascination with remembered trials of utter venture and their settings exalt them to a higher dimension of significance. The public imagination is thus kindled by these latter day Marathons and Thermopylaes, and their import takes on a like mythical character. But this reading of our modern ordeals and triumphs links them with the storied history of the past.

If there were now pilgrimages to Flanders and the Somme and to Verdun, analogous motives had prompted earlier pilgrimages to Domrémy and Reims and Chartres in honor of Jeanne d'Arc and others.

A further response to the war in the category of myth appeared also at this time in the work of poets and fabulists who appealed to such ancient protagonists of deliverance as King Arthur and Roland. This was not just a literary embroidery of the annals of war, drawing on familiar motifs from the patriotic tradition. As exemplified in David Jones' epic poem, *In Parenthesis* (rehearsing his own years at the front), this was a genuine mythopoetic transcription of the ordeal of the twentieth-century soldier in extremis as he appeals to the fortifying vision of some model from the saga of his people.

An imaginative Welsh poet, Jones orchestrates his entire portrayal of the war against the background of the myth and legend of the tribes of ancient Britain and Northern Europe. His evocation of the extremities and desperations of the war as well as its duties and motivations thus had a *cultural* grounding in image and rhetoric, which could speak across the centuries to men of this European breed. Invocation of King Arthur and his saving deeds would thus have far more than a mere literary significance.

Another example of this appeal to myth in the writing of the time by former combatants is that of the French novelist and dramatist, Henry de Montherlant. In three early writings Montherlant was devoted to defending the heroism and motives of those of his generation who served and died in the war. His own background was Mediterranean, and he looked to the classics and the annals of Rome for prototypes of the ardors and endurances of those who sought justice in like supreme confrontations in the Great War.

The justification of all such appeals to myth in interpreting the war lies in the overall continuity of our millennial struggle for some sort of viable human order, some constitution of a viable city and its defenses against violation. The vicissitudes of this ever-renewed struggle have had their recurrent similarities, and it is not surprising that in modern extremities we should look to earlier instances of heroic endurances. That they are enshrined in myth reflects that ultimate faith in the human adventure which our long quest presupposes.

At this point one may well ask what special bearing my casual and naive narrative has on these varying approaches to and retrospects on the war. To judge properly one must include my recurrent theme that this perspective is one from the ranks. (To my mind this emphasis calls attention to a special kind of stubborn fiber and keen vivacity which I associate with the common man and woman.) My journal also begins as one of a volunteer in the American Field Service and therefore as one committed to a cause identified with the embattled legacies of France and of Europe. My cumulative detail on the experience of the ranks fully recognizes, however, their frequent evasion of duty and the problems of morale and discipline in the total enterprise.

I would conclude that my early unpretentious portrayal of the war at this plebeian level confirms the view of those who see the war as an epochal drama of the European search for order and true community. It also points toward those ultimate providential securities on which we may depend for the future.

* * *

Notes

Prologue

1. A detailed portrayal of the AFS is found in the three-volume *History of the American Field Service in France* written by many of its participants (Boston: Houghton and Mifflin, 1920), hereafter *History of the American Field Service*). For recent portraits of this service and considerations of its influence on public opinion, see two articles by Andrew Gray: "Twenty-One Rue Raynouard," *French-American Review* 63, No. 1 (Spring 1992), pp. 39–43; and "The American Field Service: Volunteer Ambulances in France, World War I," *American Heritage* 26, No. 1 (December 1974), pp. 58–63, 88–92.
2. Paris, 1924, p. 38.
3. Times Literary Supplement, No. 4572, (Nov. 16–22, 1990), p. 1230.

Part I. With the American Field Service in Macedonia

1. Some details of my experience in this period as well as later in the Seventeenth Field Artillery of the American Second Division are recorded in Amos N. Wilder, "At the Nethermost Piers of History: World War I, A

View from the Ranks," in George Panichas, ed., *Promise of Greatness: The War of 1914–1918* (New York: John Day, 1968), pp. 345–357.

2. Marianne Moore, in her translation, reads more merit into the "blind venture" in question than I would claim:

> Fortune, though blind, can reward blind fearlessness
> Wisdom's impulsiveness at times earns wreaths of bay
> Though it does not pause in its impetuousness
> To visualize a means or seek out wisdom's way. (10:xiii)

The Fables of La Fontaine, trans. Marianne Moore (New York: The Viking Press, 1954), p. 253.

3. *The Handbook of Macedonia*, Geographical Section (London, 1920).

4. *History of the American Field Service*, vol. 1, "Section Three," p. 280.

5. Luigi Villari, *The Macedonian Campaign* (London, 1922), pp. 11–12.

6. See Benjamin P. Kutz's biography, *Charles Mills Galey*, (Berkeley: University of California Press, 1943), especially chapter 5, "The War Years," pp. 191–238.

7. *History of the American Field Service*, vol. 3, p. 246.

8. Sketches of this experience by Cowley and others will be found in volume 3 of the *History of the American Field Service*.

Part II. With the American Expeditionary Forces in the Field Artillery

1. Historians of America's eventual commitment to the Great War should take fuller account of this premonitory mobilization, this youth movement of that time, which early on disclosed our later course and played no insignificant part in crystallizing our total commitment. This endeavor will require thorough investigation of the history and archives of the Field Service in both its New York headquarters and the center established in France at Blérancourt maintained by the Society of Franco-American Friendship. The afterlife of the American Field Service in World War II, and the invaluable international exchange of students which thrives today, has continued to testify to the motives that presided over the origins of the Field Service.

2. "History of the Seventeenth Field Artillery, A.E.F. 1917–1918: Second Division," typescript, provides further details on this training area. The French army had acquired the tract of 23 square kilometers in 1910. Unsuitable for farming due to its stony soil, it was appropriate for artillery purposes because of its rolling hills and problems of trajectory and range finding to our officers. It was at Besançon that in 54 B.C. Caesar established his camp to oppose the tribes pressing through the Vosges and the Alsatian valley. Later, in A.D. 451, Attila set up his base at Besançon in his advance against Gaul (pp. 2–4).

3. See my poem "To G. B. and Others: Died in Action" in Amos N. Wilder, *Battle-Retrospect and Other Poems* (New Haven: Yale University Press, 1923), pp. 33–35.

4. Amos N. Wilder, *Arachne: Poems* (New Haven: Yale University Press, 1928), pp. 42–44.

5. The article, entitled "When Doughboys Turned the Tide" (*New York Times Magazine*, July 17, 1938, p. 4), is mainly concerned with the Villers-Cotterets action of this and other divisions in July, but also includes this earlier turning of the tide by our division.

6. See Wilder, *Battle-Retrospect and Other Poems*, p. 43.

✻ ✻ ✻

Index

168

✳

Index

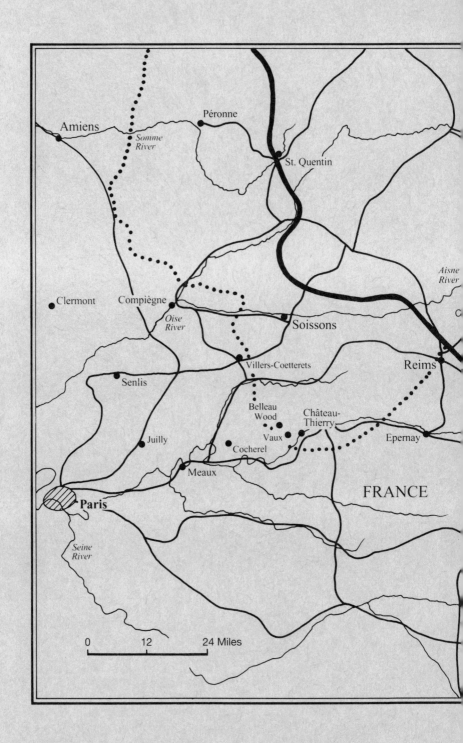

Amiens

Somme River

Péronne

St. Quentin

Aisne River

Clermont

Compiègne

Oise River

Soissons

Reims

Villers-Coetterets

Senlis

Belleau Wood

Château-Thierry

Juilly

Vaux

Epernay

Cocherel

Meaux

FRANCE

Paris

Seine River

0   12   24 Miles